THE
AMERICAN
INDIAN
WARS

⇻THE⇺
AMERICAN
INDIAN
WARS

EDWARD F. DOLAN

The Millbrook Press/Brookfield, Connecticut

Maps copyright © 2003 by Joe LeMonnier

Library of Congress Cataloging-in-Publication Data
Dolan, Edward F., 1924–
The American Indian wars / Edward F. Dolan.
p. cm.
Summary: Examines the battles and treaties between
native peoples and early European settlers of what
was to become the United States, as conflicts arose
primarily over land, but also over food and other
issues. Includes bibliographical references and index.
ISBN 0-7613-1968-9 (lib. bdg.)
1. Indians of North America—Wars—Juvenile litera-
ture. [1. Indians of North America—Wars.] I. Title.
E81 .D65 2003
973.04'97—dc21   200215301

Published by The Millbrook Press, Inc.
2 Old New Milford Road
Brookfield, CT   06804

Cover photograph courtesy of The
Granger Collection, New York

Photographs courtesy of © Corbis:
p. 3; The Granger Collection, New
York: pp. 11, 18, 19, 21, 26, 33, 35,
56, 64; The New York Public Library/
Art Resource, NY: p. 12; Library of
Congress: p. 14; North Wind Picture
Archives: pp. 22, 53, 81; Kansas State
Historical Society: p. 40; Colorado
Historical Society (CHS-X20087):
p. 45; National Archives: pp. 61, 70,
98; Denver Public Library: p. 73;
National Portrait Gallery, Smithsonian
Institution/Art Resource, NY: p. 88

CONTENTS

THE
AMERICAN
INDIAN
WARS

CHAPTER 1

WARPATHS

THE AMERICAN INDIAN WARS can be traced back to the years A.D. 1005–1007 when the Vikings tried to found a colony on the North Atlantic coast somewhere between today's New England and Labrador. The Norse attacked a group of native people there and killed eight of their number. The Norse then lost their leader, Thorvald Eriksson, when they were attacked in turn.

Some four centuries later, wherever exploration of the New World took place after the discovery in 1492, there was fighting between the newcomers and the native people. It raged northward from South America, the Caribbean Sea, and Central America to Canada and the Arctic. In the vast area that lay between, and that became the United States, the scene was bloodied for almost 400 years before the fighting at last ended in 1890 at Wounded Knee.

In this book, we'll look at those 400 years of United States upheaval. They were marked by a flood of Europeans—farmers, ranchers, traders, merchants, adventurers, household servants, and criminals—who poured westward from the Atlantic seaboard out to the Pacific coast, flowing northward to the Canadian border and southward to Mexico as they traveled. Trying to hold back the tide were the native peoples of several hundred tribes, among them the Iroquois in the East, the Sioux in the Midwest, the Apache in the Southwest, the Nez Perce in the Northwest, and the Yuma and Cayuse on the Pacific Coast.

EARLY COOPERATION

Though there was terrible trouble to come, many, if not most, tribes tried at first to live peacefully alongside the European newcomers, especially those—such as the British, French, and Dutch—who planned to settle and trade, not to plunder. They showed the new arrivals how to grow local crops. They helped them establish their first villages. And, early on, they began a healthy trade between the two groups. In all, there was a cooperation that was culturally and financially of value to both.

The Native North Americans had conducted a wide-spread trade among themselves for centuries before the arrival of the Europeans, but the newcomers brought an exchange of local products for outside goods that changed the natives' way of life. Some of the outside merchandise, such as domesticated animals and more sophisticated cooking utensils, brought changes for the good; some, chief among them alcoholic beverages, for the bad; and some, such as firearms, for a combination of good and evil.

Two of the greatest commercial products to emerge from the European-Native American acquaintance were tobacco and animal furs, especially those of the beaver. Commercial tobacco production, limited to white planters and to cultivation only in certain areas, brought little wealth to the Indians (tobacco was grown mostly by shamans, or medicine men, for health and religious purposes). Beaver furs, however, were a different matter.

Its fur in demand throughout Europe and parts of Asia for clothing—particularly for men's felt hats—the beaver was to be found almost everywhere in young America. As

Squanto, a native of the Pawtuxet tribe, teaches Pilgrims at the Plymouth Colony how to cultivate corn.

11

Dutch traders exchange goods for beaver fur at Manhattan Island (New Amsterdam, now New York). The Native American at front holds a mirror.

a result, all the major colonial powers—England, France, Russia, the Netherlands, and Spain—profited greatly in the fur traffic, with a significant share of the wealth finding its way into the hands of Indian traders and trappers.

The fur trade remained a vital part of American life for two centuries. It flourished from the whites' arrival in the 1600s until the mid-1800s.

THE CAUSES OF WAR

The trouble that would lead to war came early when the newcomers took land that was sacred to the tribes and violated it by turning it to their own uses. Later, in the wake of the Revolutionary War, the U.S. government negotiated treaties that reserved areas for native occupation, and then invited war by ignoring the pacts so that the lands could be handed over to the whites for mining, logging, ranching, and settlement.

Diseases—among them smallpox, cholera, measles, and typhus that the Europeans brought to the New World—helped to drive the tribes to war by increasing their hatred for and dread of the intruding newcomers. Because these were illnesses that had never before plagued the New World, the Native Americans had built no immunity against them. It is estimated that, by the dawn of the twentieth century, disease had reduced the native population across the United States to less than 250,000, in some cases all but wiping out entire tribes. A smallpox epidemic in 1837, for instance, was reported to have reduced the Mandan population on the upper Missouri River from 1,600 to 131. It is estimated that, prior to the 1500s, the North American native population ranged from 1 to 1.5 million people—approximately 750,000 in the future United States and 250,000 in Canada.

The Europeans not only threatened the health of the New World people but also their food supply. From the very start of the European invasion along the East Coast, there was competition between the newcomers and the Native North Americans for the croplands that had once belonged solely to the latter. Often, the competition was seen in areas where there was sufficient food for only one group or the other. Then, as the whites advanced into the Midwest, there came the tragic slaughter of the bison (widely but incorrectly known as buffalo).

The animal, a 2,000-pound (908-kilogram) giant, was an absolute necessity for tribal survival. Its flesh supplied the people with food; its skins with clothing, blankets, and

Hunting bison in the Ohio River Valley

coverings for shelter and boats; and its bones with material for tools, weapons, and cooking utensils. The bison even provided warmth, this through using their droppings—called chips or pads by all European families—as fuel for fires.

There were an estimated 40 million bison roaming the grassy plains between the Mississippi River and the Rocky Mountains when increasing numbers of whites ventured there in the 1800s. By the dawn of the twentieth century—less than one hundred years later—their number had plunged to fewer than one thousand. The greatest losses came during the years of transcontinental railroad construction in the late 1800s following the Civil War. At that time, professional hunters slaughtered vast herds to feed the work gangs laying track.

THE COMING OF WAR

In their first years in the New World, the Europeans treated the Indians with care. Care was needed because the new arrivals were greatly outnumbered by the native populations and could best survive by gaining their friendship and assistance. Soon, however, the feeling of superiority that many, if not most, of the newcomers had toward their neighbors began to show itself, bringing about the first indications of the trouble to come. Regarding the Indians as "savages," many settlers began to demand that they worship as the whites did, that they dress as the whites dressed, that they work for the whites, that they forgo their languages for those of the whites, that they surrender their lands to the whites, and that—in regard to the reservations that were taking shape across the continent—they live where the whites said they must live.

In all, the white flood threatened every aspect of Native North American life, portending the loss of everything from the Indians' ancient ways and beliefs to their identity as independent peoples. When they rose to defend themselves, the result was close to four centuries of bloody fighting.

The fighting was divided into two major phases. In the first, which began soon after the arrival of the newcomers and lasted more than two centuries, the newcomers overran the tribes living between the Atlantic coast and the Mississippi River. In the second, which began early in the nineteenth century, they cut a broad path through the tribes occupying the plains, deserts, and towering mountains—the Rockies, the Cascades, the Sierra Nevada—that lay between the Mississippi and the Pacific Coast. By the close of the second phase in 1890, the continental United States had been fully forged from east to west and from north to south.

The Indian domination of the continent had come to an end. Life would never again be for them what it had been for centuries.

CHAPTER 2

THE FIRST BATTLES

ROM THEIR EARLIEST DAYS in the New World, the Spanish and British met native resistance wherever they went. Throughout the 1500s, the people of South, Central, and North America everywhere resisted the Spanish advance. The British met the same resistance soon after arriving in North America late in the century. It struck as they put down their first roots along the Atlantic coast.

The trouble came in the year 1622. The Powhatan of the future states of Virginia and Maryland began what became a fourteen-year war against the settlers in their midst. The fighting erupted in March when the Indians attacked the tobacco farms that the newcomers had built around the village of Jamestown. Killed in the fighting were 347 settlers. The village itself, heavily fortified, went untouched.

Why the attack? When the British had first come ashore and founded Jamestown in 1607, a mere fifteen years earlier, the Powhatan had welcomed them. But soon the Indians were angered by several problems. Among them were charges that the settlers had unfairly taken some of the Powhatan lands and had also caused a drain on the local food supply.

The settlers were accused of failing to plant food crops for themselves. Instead, they had devoted much of their

In 1622, in what became known as the Jamestown Massacre, Powhatan Indians attacked settlements around Jamestown, Virginia.

THE PRINCESS NAMED POCAHONTAS

This engraving shows Pocahontas, a Powhatan princess, bringing corn to the colonists at Jamestown, Virginia.

One of the most famous women in early American history—perhaps *the* most famous—was the princess Pocahontas. Born in the final decade of the 1500s, she was the daughter of the chief of the Powhatan.

Bearing the tribal name Matoaka, she found her place in early American history during the first years of the British presence in Virginia. It happened when Captain John Smith, who had helped to establish the settlement at Jamestown, was captured by the Powhatan in 1608 and was brought to the village where Pocahontas lived. There, Smith was said to have been placed before a stone altar to be killed, only to be saved when the young princess threw herself on his body and successfully pleaded for his life.

Today, many historians doubt the story and look on it as legend. But no one doubts that Pocahontas obviously wanted to improve the uneasy relations between the Powhatan and the English in their midst. She worked hard to keep peace between the two groups, with one of her greatest successes coming when she convinced her father to provide the colonists with food when they were starving.

Nor is there any doubt that she lived a fascinating life during those years. In 1614, after learning the ways of the English and mastering their language, she married a successful tobacco planter named John Rolfe and bore him a son. Then, in 1616, she sailed to England with her family and a group of Powhatan servants. There, she was entertained by royalty and members of the country's aristocracy.

Her visit, however, ended in sadness. In 1617, during her preparations to return home, Pocahontas fell ill and died. She was buried in England, where her grave marker still stands. She was in her mid-twenties at the time.

land to growing tobacco for export to Europe, where its popularity was quickly spreading. As a result, they had put too heavy a strain on the Indians' food supply.

The Virginia fighting, marked by an English attack that claimed one thousand Powhatan lives, continued until the Indians were subdued in 1636. They rose again in 1644, threatened Jamestown, and killed between four hundred and five hundred whites in a series of attacks before being defeated for a final time in 1644.

1600S: KING PHILIP'S WAR

Fifty-three years after the outbreak of fighting at Jamestown and far to the north, the most destructive of the early Indian wars occurred in June 1675. It began when warriors of the Wampanoag tribe raided the village of Swansea in New England's Plymouth Colony. The conflict that followed was called King Philip's War, named for a chief of the Wampanoag. His tribal name was Metacom, but he was widely known to the British colonists as King Philip.

Like the Powhatan, Philip had once been a friend of the British, but he had turned against them as their numbers increased and their influence spread throughout his domain and those of neighboring tribes. He attacked the village of Swansea soon after the foreigners charged three of his people with the murder of a colonial employee and executed them.

The Swansea raid loosed a war that spread from Plymouth to the colonies of Massachusetts Bay, Connecticut, Rhode Island, New Hampshire, and Maine. It soon involved a number of local native groups, among them the Nipmuck and Pocumtuck. One neutral tribe, the Narragansett of Rhode Island, suffered the greatest loss when, in late 1675, a British force of 1,200 men attacked a tribal fort, set it afire, and slaughtered several hundred adults and children.

For their part, Philip's warriors and their allies raged through Massachusetts for months, attacking the settlements of Brookfield, Sudbury, Deerfield, and Lancaster. They killed most of Lancaster's male population and took all its women and children prisoner.

The burning of Brookfield, Massachusetts, during King Philip's War, 1675

Major George Washington, in camp during the French and Indian War, leads his troops in prayers.

The American Indians were caught up in two major conflicts fought during the 1600s and 1700s by the whites in their midst—the French and Indian Wars and the American Revolution.

The French and Indian Wars consisted of four conflicts that raged between England and France and their allies from 1689 to 1763. Known in America as King William's War, Queen Anne's War, King George's War, and the French and Indian War, they were the New World offshoots of conflicts between the two countries in Europe.

When the fighting began, both nations were major powers in the Americas. At their close, however, France had lost much of its New World empire to Great Britain — Canada and all the possessions east of the Mississippi River down to just outside the city of New Orleans. Also in British hands was the former Spanish possession that would one day include the U.S. state of Florida.

Waged between 1776 and 1782, the American Revolution broke England's hold on its New World colonies and ended in the establishment of the United States.

Caught up in both conflicts were many Indian nations. For example, in Queen Anne's War, six New England groups that made up a major Indian alliance called the Abenaki Confederacy were allied with the French. Another group, the Iroquois, sided with the English.

In King George's War, the French sought the military support of the Choctaw, Cherokee, and Creek tribes. They succeeded in winning over the Choctaw and some Creek to their side, but they failed to win the backing of the Cherokee.

The French and Indian War gave American history one of its most famous incidents, a clash that took shape in 1755 when 1,450 British under the command of General Edward Braddock marched out from Fort Cumberland (in present-day Maryland) to capture Fort Duquesne (today's Pittsburgh, Pennsylvania). En route, Braddock was ambushed by an enemy force of about eight hundred Indians, Frenchmen, and Canadians. Striking without warning from behind trees and bushes, they inflicted heavy casualties on Braddock's troops and dealt the general himself a mortal wound.

A portion of his command was helped, however, by a company of Americans headed by a young George Washington. Washington and his men hampered the Indian attack and led the British survivors — fewer than five hundred men — back to the safety of Fort Cumberland.

Involved in the Revolutionary War years later were the members of the giant Iroquois League of Six Nations. But they were split in their loyalties, with four members choosing to ally with the British and two with the Americans. Siding with the British were the Mohawk, Onondaga, Cayuga, and Seneca tribes, while the Oneida and Tuscarora joined the Americans.

Regardless of which side they supported, the Indians who fought in the Revolutionary War suffered for their participation when peace finally came. When arranging the peace treaty at war's end, the defeated British did not insist on provisions that would ensure the proper treatment of the nations that had supported them. Nor did the Americans offer any special treatment to their Native American supporters. All tribes, both those who had aided and those who had opposed the Americans, were treated as a single group.

The war's principal fighting ended in August 1676 when an Indian in the employ of the British shot and killed Philip. But hostilities continued until a formal peace was reached the next year after British forces had wiped out the remaining Indian bands. The fighting cost the lives of six hundred British troops, while the New England tribes lost much of the political and military power they had long held.

1700S: FIGHTING IN THE OLD NORTHWEST

Soon after the close of the Revolutionary War, the infant United States began urging its people to settle certain of the frontier lands that had been won from Great Britain. Spreading through what was known as the Old Northwest—the home of today's Ohio, Indiana, Illinois, Wisconsin, and sections of Michigan—these lands stretched out to the Mississippi River and were occupied by a number of allied Indian groups, chief among them the Shawnee, Delaware (Lennai Lenape), and Miami.

When the Americans began arriving there in the 1780s, the Indians set about driving them off by attacking their farms and settlements. Behind many of the attacks were British troops who had refused to leave the area after losing the Revolutionary War and who had continued to supply arms to the tribes.

The attacks were at first successful. So were the later battles with the American troops who had arrived to snuff out the trouble. In a 1791 fight, for example, a 1,400-man force under Major General Arthur St. Clair suffered 913 casualties, the worst defeat ever to be handed to an American force by Indian warriors.

But the Indians were doomed to eventual defeat. It came in 1794 when they were decisively beaten by U.S. troops in the Battle of Fallen Timbers, named for an Ohio spot where the trees had been uprooted by a violent wind-

TWO CALLS FOR INDIAN UNITY:
PONTIAC AND TECUMSEH

Two of the most powerful figures to oppose the spreading influence of foreigners westward from the Atlantic coastline were the Ottawa leader Pontiac (c. 1720–1768) and the Shawnee chieftain Tecumseh (c. 1768–1813). Both did, early on, what few Native American leaders were able to do at any time—unite various tribal groups into single bodies to oppose the spread of whites.

Their efforts were to fail, but nevertheless earned them lasting places in the annals of the Native American struggle against the white invasion.

PONTIAC

Pontiac's story begins in 1760 when the British defeated the French in the French and Indian War and took over the territory called the Old Northwest.

Immediately following their victory, the British stopped a longtime practice of supplying the surrounding Indian groups with food, saying that it was of no genuine value in controlling the Native Americans. The action both alarmed and angered the recipients, and matters only worsened when the new victors began to grant some Indian lands in the eastern area of the Old Northwest to British officers who had done especially valuable service in the war.

Though the Native American groups all shared the same anger, they remained as they had been for a long while—independent bodies that had never combined for greater strength when fighting a common enemy. But the time was at hand for a leader who could take them in that direction, and he emerged in the person of the Ottawa chieftain Pontiac. In all ways an impressive figure—a speaker, a warrior, and a man of vision—Pontiac began the task of uniting the various peoples in the region of the Great Lakes and the Ohio Valley.

He won supporters wherever he went by voicing the teachings of the Native American preacher Neolin (meaning "the Enlightened One"), who was better known among his listeners as the Delaware Prophet. Neolin called for the native people to return to their traditional values and to avoid all that was modern and foreign, including the use of firearms.

With the exception of the ban on firearms, Pontiac embraced Neolin's teachings and, with them as a rallying force, developed a loose confederation of the local tribes. He then led the confederation in attacks against the British in 1763, all meant to drive the hated enemy out. His forces captured eight forts and severed various British supply lines.

Chief Pontiac in council with the elders of his Ottawa tribe

Pontiac's efforts were supported by the French in his area, but were doomed to failure with the news that French troops elsewhere were capitulating and withdrawing from North America to leave the British in control. Pontiac's rebellion collapsed, but it did result in a British agreement to prohibit settlers from moving into Seneca lands west of the Appalachian Mountains.

Pontiac's life ended as suddenly and tragically as his campaign against the British. He was clubbed and stabbed to death by a fellow Indian at Chakia, Illinois, on April 30, 1769. It is thought that the murder was committed in retaliation for the death of an Indian at Pontiac's hands three years earlier.

As did Pontiac's attacks against the British end in failure, so did his confederation of tribes. The struggle to halt the westward advance of the whites was then taken up by Tecumseh.

TECUMSEH

Throughout his life, Tecumseh fought to stop the spreading white settlement of Indian land. In the Old Northwest, he did battle with the troops of generals Arthur St. Clair and "Mad" Anthony Wayne. He then refused to sign the 1795 Treaty of Greenville.

Next, on watching with growing alarm the flood of white settlers out to the Mississippi River, Tecumseh in 1809 issued a call to all the tribes living between Canada in the north and the Gulf of Mexico in the south. He urged them to unite against the mounting white flood by joining him in the formation of an Indian confederation to resist the further loss of their lands. In teachings similar to those of Pontiac, he urged the tribes to ensure success by putting aside old hatreds and rivalries, pledging never to sell land that all Indians held in common, and cooperating with one another.

In the War of 1812, Tecumseh sided with the British against the United States. He was named a brigadier general, commanding two thousand Shawnee troops, and played a role in the capture of Fort Detroit. His call for Indian unity against the white invasion won many supporters, but came to a sudden end with his death during the 1813 Battle of the Thames.

storm some years earlier. The Americans were commanded by the Revolutionary War hero, General "Mad" Anthony Wayne. The victory led to the 1795 Treaty of Greenville. In the pact, the Indians agreed to let the whites settle the southern two thirds of the Old Northwest.

1800S: THE PLIGHT OF THE "FIVE CIVILIZED TRIBES"

The people of what were called the Five Civilized Tribes occupied a vast southeastern area of the United States in the early 1800s. Their tribes were the Cherokee, Chickasaw, Choctaw, Creek, and Seminole. They totaled some one hundred thousand people and were to be found in Florida Territory and at least four states—Alabama, Georgia, Mississippi, and Tennessee.

They were widely known as the Five Civilized Tribes because they early on adopted the ways of the Europeans who settled near them. As a result, in the eyes of the newcomers, they lived a more "civilized" life than did other tribes. They had long farmed and traded for their livelihood. Now they adopted European dress, European-style houses, and, eventually, European codes of law.

Though the Indians were said to be much like the whites, there was still fighting between the two groups for years. For example, the Creek (also known as Muskogee) resisted the white settlement of Georgia and Alabama in the early nineteenth century. Their resistance led to a war that erupted in 1811 and ended three years later in the Battle of Horseshoe Bend in today's Alabama. The fighting claimed the lives of over seven hundred Creek braves. Just as the U.S. Army had suffered its greatest loss of men at Indian hands in 1791, so now did Horseshoe Bend mark the worst Indian battlefield defeat ever at army hands.

THE RESERVATION SYSTEM
AND THE ERA OF TREATIES

The idea of placing Native Americans on reservations dates back to the seventeenth century, when, in 1638, the Puritans of New England set aside acreage in the future state of Connecticut for the exclusive use of the Algonquian-speaking group.

The plan at that time was not to share the land more peaceably by separating the Indians from the whites, but to separate the Algonquian people from those of a tribal enemy. The idea of setting aside acreage for exclusive use by the Indians to protect them from white encroachments did not take root until after the Revolutionary War. It was first put to use with the granting of a reservation in western New York State to the Iroquois.

By the mid-1800s, reservations were being formed for a dual purpose—first, to keep the lands safe from a mounting white invasion and, second, to establish places where the Indians could be instructed in white customs and work methods so that one day they could take their places in an increasingly non-Indian society.

Located in what would become the New England and eastern states, the first reservations were small in size because of the nature of the regions. They assumed gigantic proportions when the nation moved into the sprawling lands beyond the Mississippi River, first with the establishment of Indian Territory in the 1830s and then (as will be described in Chapter 5) in the wake of the Civil War, with the Great Sioux Reservation farther west. The sizes of many reservations were reduced, however, when the land could not be kept safe from invasion and development as masses of white

Over a span of twenty-four years in the nineteenth century, the Seminole of Florida fought two wars with the United States, the first during 1817 and 1818, and the second between 1835 and 1842. At the time of the 1817–1818 outbreak, Florida was a Spanish possession and served as a goal for slaves fleeing from U.S. plantations. Along with the fugitives, Florida also sheltered gangs of Seminole and whites—many of whom would attack plantations and settlements in neighboring Georgia and then vanish back across the border to safety.

settlers swept westward to the Pacific shores. Treaties that had established the reservations were altered, or their terms ignored, as the advance rolled forward, infuriating the Indians and making them distrustful of the U.S. government.

The government's official tool for dealing with Indian matters between 1778 and 1871, when its use was ended, was the treaty. In that time, over 370 treaties were negotiated and signed. In addition to founding reservations and then altering their size when necessary, the treaties dealt with such matters as:

The settlement of wars
The award of railroad rights-of-way across Indian territory
The surrender of lands to the United States
The establishment of trade agreements with the federal government

Government negotiators offered various terms to Indians who signed the pacts. They ranged from the provision of food, money, schooling, and medical care to the right to hunt, fish, and farm the land in question as long as the signers remained at peace.

Even though the United States officially ended its use of the treaty in 1871, the federal government negotiated some seventy-five additional land and other agreements with the Native Americans. The last one was signed early in the twentieth century.

The situation drove the American government to send Major General Andrew Jackson and a three-thousand-man army into Florida to put an end to the trouble over there. His campaign proved a success and led Spain to hand the region to the United States in 1819. Congress then set aside—reserved—a 4-million-acre (1.6-million-hectare) Florida tract for Indian use only. Located on the region's poorest land, it was a "gift" that infuriated the Indians. Their anger worsened when Florida was soon invaded by hordes of U.S. settlers.

The Seminole resisted the invasion, beginning with a December 1835 attack on an army detachment that left 108 of its soldiers dead. Fighting continued through the next years with skirmishes and pitched battles. In one of the latter, a future American president, Colonel Zachary Taylor, hurled several hundred troops against a Seminole position on Christmas Day 1837, and sustained 138 casualties before managing to uproot the defenders.

At last, in 1842, the Seminole suffered their final defeat. They then had to watch as 4,000 of their tribe's 4,800 people were made to trudge west across the Mississippi River to what was called Indian Territory. The territory consisted of land that the federal government had just set aside for Indian use only. The eight hundred who remained behind had long been hiding from the American authorities.

1800S: INDIAN TERRITORY

The story of Indian Territory dated back to 1825 and President James Monroe's suggestion that all tribes living east of the Mississippi River be moved by the U.S. government to some unpopulated region west of the waterway. The disruption would be great, yes, but Monroe argued that it would spare the country—and the Indians themselves— the agony of future wars over the increasing white settlement and development of the nation's lands.

In 1830, President Andrew Jackson carried Monroe's suggested plan a step further. He proposed the Indian Removal Act to Congress. On becoming law, the measure would set aside vast acreage to the west of the Mississippi River for Indian use. Second, the act would authorize Congress to allot $500,000 to pay the Indians for their lost homelands and to help finance their resettlement.

The proposed act met with mixed public reaction. It was strongly supported by white settlers, farmers, plantation owners, and various business people, all knowing that it would clear millions of acres for them to develop. Other Americans vehemently condemned the whole idea. The act, they charged, was nothing more than outright theft by the U.S. government.

In the face of such divided opinion, Congress passed the act by only a slim margin—103 to 97. The measure was then signed into law by President Jackson on May 28, 1830.

The peaceful Choctaw were the first to travel westward to their new grounds, a journey of 400 miles (644 kilometers) from their home in the state of Mississippi. About 13,000 made the trip between the winter of 1830 and the last march in 1834, some walking, some riding in wagons. Some froze to death in the harsh cold. They left behind 10.5 million acres (4.3 million hectares) of tribal land for white use. Following close behind, in 1832, came the defeated Creek and then, in the 1840s, the Seminole.

In addition to the two Seminole wars mentioned earlier, a few members of the tribe fought a third war when they refused a U.S. order to leave Florida for Indian Territory. Provoked by the growing number of outsiders who were building settlements and roads on Indian land, the war began with an attack on an army post in December 1855 and ended with a major Seminole defeat in March 1857.

1800S: THE CHEROKEE TRAGEDY

A presidential request in the mid-1830s resulted in tragedy for the Cherokee tribe. That year, President Andrew Jackson asked Congress to move the Cherokee from their Georgia and North Carolina homes to Indian Territory. He made the request at the urging of the white settlers who wanted the tribe gone so that the Georgia land could be used "more efficiently."

Actually, the government had no legal grounds for seeking the removal of the Cherokee to Indian Territory. Though they lived east of the Mississippi, they were protected from the move by three treaties that the tribe had signed with the young United States in the late 1700s. All three stipulated that whites could never settle on Cherokee lands. Unwittingly, the government signers had made it impossible for anyone to oust the Cherokee by means of the Indian Removal Act.

Nevertheless, Congress approved Jackson's request in 1835. Some 16,000 Cherokee were occupying lands in Georgia when they received the notice to leave. Later, on hearing that only 2,000 of their number had traveled west by 1838, newly elected President Martin Van Buren ordered General Winfield Scott to move the rest of the tribe immediately. Scott marched 7,000 troops into Georgia and herded the Cherokee into army stockades in Georgia and across the border in Tennessee. Then he forced more than 2,500 of their number—men, women, and children—to lead the 850-mile (1,369-kilometer) march out to their new "homeland" with the remaining families soon to follow. When many of the Cherokee still housed in the stockades fell ill in the summer heat, Scott agreed to delay their departure until cooler weather set in. They then trudged westward between late August and early December.

The removal cost the tribe some four thousand lives, with most of the deaths occurring not on the road but in the stockades. Their march and the others that then followed were called one of the greatest harms—if not *the* greatest—ever inflicted on a minority population by the U.S. government, earning the haunting name "The Trail of Tears."

"The Trail of Tears," the forced march of the Cherokee in 1838

By the mid-1840s, the bulk of the trouble east of the Mississippi River had ended. The tribes there had been defeated, with most now living on lands reserved for them through treaties with the federal government. Now lying ahead and facing the migrating whites were the vast lands that stretched west from the river to the Rocky Mountains and then on to the Pacific coast. They were to be the next great battlefields in the American Indian Wars.

CHAPTER 3

DEEP INTO THE WEST

PRIOR TO THE 1840S, the lands beyond the Mississippi River were little known to the white settlers. Only a few adventurers had visited them. Once or twice a year, starting in the 1820s, bands of traders moved their wagon trains along the Santa Fe Trail, a rutted pathway that ran from Missouri to the town of Santa Fe in the future state of New Mexico, there to sell their wares to the Mexican citizens. Handfuls of trappers and hunters searched for beaver (whose fur was the source of the internationally popular beaver felt hat) in the Rocky Mountains and the wilderness lands farther west. The region boasted a few trading posts and army forts.

The trails to the Far West were also few in number. One major roadway, the Oregon Trail, stretched from Missouri out to Oregon Country, the fertile region that would one day become the states of Oregon and Washington. Branching away from it at one point was the California Trail, which, true to its name, snaked its way southwest into California.

The two trails, however, suddenly began to handle an increasing number of migrating newcomers in the 1840s. Luring settlers to Oregon Country and California were reports of the fine climates and rich farmlands there on the Pacific coast. Oregon, which had attracted a mere 125 settlers in 1842, drew 875 in 1843, with the annual totals then mounting steadily to 2,500 in 1845 and 4,000 in 1847.

Covered wagons and stagecoaches on the Oregon Trail in Wyoming

Though impressive, these figures couldn't match those recorded by the California Trail, an astonishing 25,500 in 1849 alone, as hordes of Americans—from farmers to gamblers—stampeded west in search of the gold that had been discovered on the west side of the Sierra Nevada Mountains. The number ballooned in the next year, aided by an additional 100,000 who reached California by sea from the Atlantic seaboard, Europe, and Asia.

At first, the mounting numbers of wagon trains rumbling west from the Mississippi and Missouri Rivers did not alarm most of the Indians in their path. After all, the wagons were simply passing through on their way to distant destinations. The tribes were usually content to help the travelers along, pointing the way ahead and hopefully getting rid of them for good.

Some tribes, with a sharp eye for a profit, charged the trains a toll—food, animals, or trinkets—in exchange for the promise of safe passage across their lands. In 1851 the U.S. government took a step to end the Indian-white bargaining that had easily led to exploding tempers and violence. It promised to pay the Indians for any hunting spoils and for other losses to the newcomers so long as the tribes let them pass across the land unmolested.

For the first years of the 1840s, there was only scattered trouble between the Native Americans and the westward-bound pioneers. Then, beginning late in the decade and extending through the 1850s, trouble was to be seen everywhere, especially in the Far West—in the gold rush of California.

TROUBLE IN CALIFORNIA

The events of the 1850s and 1860s—as the gold seekers poured into the state—cost the California Indians thousands of lives. It was a continuation of a pattern of death that began back in 1769 with the arrival of the Spanish. At the start of the Spanish era, California's Indian population had totaled about 300,000. By 1849, the opening year of the gold rush, that number had fallen to around 150,000, a drop caused principally by the arrival of European diseases that the population had never before suffered— among them, malaria, smallpox, and cholera.

The hordes of gold-rush miners then caused widespread hunger in the native population as they overran the Indian hunting and gathering grounds and began to pirate the Indians' food. In the San Francisco Bay region alone, white hunters turned a handsome profit by killing thousands of ducks, rabbits, and deer and then peddling them in San Francisco, Sacramento, and dozens of Sierra gold camps.

From its very start, several tribes fought the settlers' invasion in both northern and southern California, among them the Miwok and Yokut in the Sierra foothills of the north, and the Yuma (Quechan) far to the south near the border with Mexico's Baja California.

While clashes with the army troops guarding the territories were often no more than skirmishes, the white miners themselves were soon waging an undeclared war on the tribes. They formed militia units for Indian hunts, financing the searches with funds provided by the state government (California joined the Union in September 1850). Singly or in small groups, the whites gunned down Indians for the bounty that was paid for their scalps.

All the tragedy—the starvation, the diseases, and the fighting—exacted a terrible cost from the California Indians. They lost some 115,000 lives between 1850 and 1860, a drop in the native population from 150,000 to between 30,000 and 35,000.

TROUBLE IN THE NORTHWEST

The 1850s were also marked by warfare in the Pacific Northwest. In 1855, in Washington Territory (which would become a state in 1889), Governor Isaac Stevens called the Indian tribes of the region to a conference at the settlement of Walla Walla. Among those attending were the leaders of the Cayuse, Nez Perce, Walla Walla, and Yakima (also spelled Yakama) tribes.

They heard Stevens ask them to relinquish their tribal lands in exchange for reservations and various payments, among them homes, cattle, money for their families, and schools for their children. Stevens promised that, if they

DEATH AT WALLA WALLA

Marcus Whitman and his wife, Narcissa, were Presbyterian missionaries who had traveled west along the Oregon Trail in 1836 to settle near present-day Walla Walla, Washington. On their arrival, they founded a mission for the Cayuse tribe and then labored there for the next eleven years. The Cayuse looked on Marcus as a powerful healer and, because they had never seen a white woman before, thought Narcissa to be a white goddess.

But their admiration suddenly ended in 1847, and it was replaced by a deep hatred. Causing the trouble was an epidemic of measles that, triggered by a passing wagon train, spread through the mission and took the lives of many of its children. When Marcus was helpless to save the youngsters, the terrified Indians began to think that he was trying to get rid of the tribe so that he could take over its lands.

Their blind fear drove them to attack the mission and burn it to the ground. Left dead among the ashes were the Whitmans, along with ten of their white workers.

The murders enraged the surrounding settlers. They raised a local military force and attacked an encampment of Cayuse who had played no part in the mission tragedy. About thirty died at white hands, driving the various tribes for miles around to strike back. The militia finally called a halt to the fighting, but not before the region's Native Americans, who had long enjoyed peaceful relations with the whites, had learned to distrust all outsiders.

As a result, the Cayuse themselves were to be involved in various struggles, among them the Yakima War of 1855–58, for years to come.

accepted his offer, they would not have to move to the reservations for at least two years.

The offer was a tempting one at a time when all the tribes were feeling the terrible crush of the settlers pouring into the territory—tempting enough to win the acceptance of some. But, less than two weeks after their acceptance had resulted in a signed treaty, Stevens infuriated the Indians by declaring the lands immediately open to white settlement. It was an announcement that led to some three years of fighting.

The violence began when five Yakima tribesmen assaulted and killed six gold prospectors and triggered the Yakima War of 1855 and 1856. The fighting spread south into Oregon, where U.S. troops, fearful that a revolt was brewing among the Takelma and Tututni people, attacked one of their villages, slaughtering twenty-three women, children, and old men. The young men of the village, away at the time of the slaughter, soon retaliated by ambushing a force of white soldiers. Other tribes then staged uprisings in 1856, when one thousand of their warriors combined for an attack on the settlement of Seattle, only to be driven off by cannon fire from a ship in Puget Sound.

ON THE EVE OF THE CIVIL WAR

The Pacific coast was far from being the only scene of Indian-white tensions in 1861, the eve of the Civil War. Everywhere west of the Mississippi there was friction between the Native Americans and the growing hordes of whites—not only the settlers but increasing numbers of army troops who arrived to guard them and build a string of forts for the protection of the roadways.

For instance, the theft of a cow belonging to a group of Mormon settlers ended in an 1854 tragedy in Wyoming. When the Mormons accused the Brule (a branch of the Lakota Sioux) of stealing the thin, aged, and starved-looking animal, an army unit attempted to make an arrest only to find itself entangled in a fight that cost twenty-eight soldiers and a civilian worker their lives. Called the Grattan Massacre for the commander of the army unit—Lieutenant John Grattan—the incident led to an 1855 battle in which the army avenged the deaths by killing eighty-five Brule men and taking seventy women and children captive.

In 1857 the army sent a three-hundred-man mounted unit in search of the Cheyenne to punish them for attacking settlers who were heading into the Rocky Mountains. Among those who died in the attacks were gold prospectors, trappers, and a stagecoach driver. The troop found the Indians in western Kansas in late July and routed them in a cavalry charge.

Some of the last Indian fighting prior to the Civil War erupted in Nevada in 1860 when the Paiute of the Pyramid Lake region flew into a rage on learning that two of their young women had been kidnapped and raped by silver miners at a nearby trading post. A band of Paiute warriors attacked the post and rescued the two young women, burning the place to the ground and killing seven whites in the process.

Western Indians, without benefit of rifles, besiege a covered wagon in this illustration from the 1850s.

A force of eight hundred miners and a contingent of U.S. infantry from Nevada and California sought out the attackers and killed twenty-five of their number in two battles, before the Indians scattered into the surrounding mountains. On being tracked down, the Paiute were exiled to a reservation.

THE CIVIL WAR YEARS

When the Civil War at last exploded in 1861, it brought a degree of peace to the West. First, the war caused the white expansion westward to slow. Second, the federal troops serving on the frontier were shifted to the battle sites in the North and South, to be replaced by local—and often inexperienced and inefficient—volunteer outfits. (Many historians think that the tribes could have further delayed the white expansion had they been able to unify at this time and fight as a single force. But they were never able to do so.)

Despite the slowing white expansion, there were still outbreaks of violence in or en route to the West. In the Minnesota of early 1861, the Santee of the Sioux were angered when white men came flooding across their land to reach the newly discovered gold fields in Montana. In addition, there was the rumor that money payments and food shipments promised to the Santee by the U.S. government were to be canceled. When the tribal leaders requested additional food from a local storekeeper, he coldly told them to "eat grass."

The tension mounted through the months and finally exploded into open warfare in August. Led by Chief Little Crow, the Santee attacked various settlements and took the lives of more than eight hundred settlers, scalping many and mutilating their bodies. Among the victims was a trader whose corpse was found with grass stuffed in its mouth.

When U.S. Army troops struck back in fury, they crushed the uprising in a month, taking several hundred prisoners in the process. A military commission then sentenced 303 of the captives to death. President Abraham Lincoln, touched by the hardships that had driven the Santee to war, commuted the death sentence of all but 38 of the men. The 38 were publicly hanged on December 26, 1862.

The Santee who survived the brief war left Minnesota. Most finally settled on a reservation in the future state of Nebraska. But many shunned reservation life. They joined with the great Sioux leader, Sitting Bull, and so were destined to face U.S. troops in battle again.

Chief Little Crow escaped execution, but did not flee Minnesota. He was shot and killed by a farmer in 1863 when he and his son—starving—were sighted picking berries on the farmer's land.

A year later a tragedy befell the Navajo of Arizona, New Mexico, and Utah when a Union army force under General James Carleton and Colonel Kit Carson arrived and set about pacifying the tribe so that it would not interfere with Union efforts in the war. The troops burned homes, crops, and livestock everywhere, driving some six thousand Navajo to surrender by early 1864. The captives were then marched 350 miles (564 kilometers) to a reservation on New Mexico's Pecos River, with two thousand more arriving some months later. They remained at the camp, sick and starving, until 1868. They were finally allowed to return home after signing away most of their lands to the federal government.

The Shoshone of today's Idaho, Wyoming, and Utah spent the Civil War years meeting the settlers' invasion of their lands by attacking stagecoaches, wagon trains, and even the Pony Express riders of 1860 and 1861. To put a stop to the attacks, a troop of three hundred volunteers struck a Shoshone village and killed over two hundred of its people. Afterward, this tribe too was forced to sign a treaty in which it turned over much of its land to the federal government.

The final full year of the war, 1864, was marked by a new brutality—the Sand Creek Massacre—that opened the door to two years of vicious Indian–white fighting.

THE SAND CREEK MASSACRE

The story of the massacre began with the 1858 discovery of gold in Colorado. Some 100,000 white miners surged into the territory. They inspired the territorial governor, John Evans, to entice them to stay on as settlers after the gold fever ended. To do so, Evans set about trying to buy the hunting grounds of the Cheyenne and Arapaho for use as farmlands. The two groups refused to sell and also balked at settling on the reservation that had been established for them alongside the Sand Creek River in southeastern Colorado.

Evans next tried to win the lands through violence. He sent Colonel John Chivington, the commander of the territory's volunteer army forces (now serving in the absence of regular troops), against the Cheyenne and Arapaho. They responded to his attacks with attacks of their own. Joined by Sioux, Comanche, and Kiowa friends, they spent the summer of 1864 rampaging throughout Colorado and neighboring Kansas, attacking mining camps, wagon trains, and farmers tilling their fields.

As winter approached, several Cheyenne and Arapaho chiefs called for a meeting with Evans and Chivington. The chiefs had long opposed the attacks by their warriors and now wanted to talk peace. Leading them was the Cheyenne chief, Black Kettle.

Evans and Chivington told Black Kettle that, before any peace talks could be held, he would have to convince his braves to end their attacks and surrender their arms. When the chief accepted these terms, he was told to make camp at Sand Creek while arrangements were completed for the talks. Chivington, however, had long nursed a deep hatred for all Indians, believing that they would never keep any agreements made with whites. Consequently, instead of preparing for the conference, he quietly gathered his militia troops and led them to the Sand Creek encampment. Seven hundred strong, they were all volunteers who had started life in Colorado as gold miners. They shared his hatred of Indians.

At dawn on November 29, 1864, the troops suddenly appeared on the bluffs above the camp. Below, some five hundred Cheyenne men, women, and children, along with fifty Arapaho friends, were just awakening. Bewildered, they stared up at the Americans. Black Kettle, thinking that some terrible mistake was in the making, quickly raised an American flag and a white banner of surrender above his tepee. But there was no mistake. As rifle and howitzer fire poured in on the victims from above, Chivington's cavalry swept down into the encampment. The tragedy that befell Black Kettle and his people in the next minutes was later described by an eyewitness, an interpreter named John Smith:

> They were scalped, their brains knocked out; the men used their knives, ripped open women, clubbed little children, knocked them in the head with their guns, beat their brains out, mutilated their bodies in every sense of the word.

Chivington claimed that over 450 Indians lost their lives in a matter of minutes, a count that was later adjusted to approximately 200. Two thirds of the dead were said to be women and children. Black Kettle himself survived the massacre. He lived another four years before losing his life in 1868 fighting with U.S. cavalry troops.

The Sand Creek Massacre on November 29, 1864

During those years, the Cheyenne, with the help of Sioux, Arapaho, and Kiowa friends, avenged the dead at Sand Creek with raids on stagecoaches, stage stations, ranches, and mines throughout Colorado, plus raids in neighboring Kansas. An attack on Julesburg, Colorado, left the town in ashes.

The attacks were marked by Indian brutalities meant to match those of Chivington's men. On one occasion, the Cheyenne were said to have forced a wire from ear to ear through the head of a telegrapher who had died at their hands. The Indians, knowing that the Americans could talk to one another through a wire, had brutalized his corpse so that he could hear better throughout eternity.

The Indians were not alone in their outrage over the Sand Creek slaughter. The U.S. government shared their fury and, in 1868, assigned a commission to investigate the matter. Named to the group were influential civilians and three of the army's most distinguished officers—generals William Tecumseh Sherman, C. C. Auger, and Alfred H. Terry. After studying the raid, the commission unanimously condemned the action, declaring:

> It scarcely has its parallel in the records of Indian barbarity. Fleeing women, holding up their hands and praying for mercy, were shot down; infants were killed and scalped in derision; men were tortured and scalped . . .

Following the commission's study, Chivington resigned from the army to escape facing a court-martial. He never expressed regret for the attack.

In response to all the Indian revenge, the U.S. Army had, in 1865, sent General John Pope and six thousand troops in search of the Cheyenne and their allies. It was a hunt that ended in failure. The Indians easily evaded his troops, who were slowed by their long lines of supply wagons.

Then, in the winter of 1868, with the Civil War now three years in the past, the army launched a new campaign, this one against the Cheyenne alone. Its aim was to intimidate the tribe by moving against them in winter, a time when they had always believed that the weather made them safe from attack.

Into the field went a force consisting of three separate columns. One was a mounted unit—the 7th Cavalry—under the command of Lieutenant Colonel George Armstrong Custer, who had won widespread fame for his successful actions in the Civil War. In November 1868 he located the winter camp of Black Kettle on the Washita River in today's Oklahoma.

Custer attacked in the predawn of November 27. Spearing in from two directions, his riders killed 100 adults and children, slaughtered a herd of 120 ponies, captured 53 women and children, and burned the camp to the ground. When Black Kettle and his wife attempted an escape on horseback, they were fatally shot by the soldiers.

The attacks, on being reported in the press, added to the fame that Custer had won throughout the North during the Civil War and established him in the minds of many Americans as a dashing and superb Indian fighter. He was to die seven years later while assaulting another Indian encampment, this one on the Little Bighorn River in Montana Territory.

The next chapter returns us to the years immediately before the Civil War and takes place in the Southwest, in the sunbaked lands of the Apache people. Marked by vicious fighting, the decades that followed were to be imprinted with the names of two of the greatest warriors in Apache—and United States—history.

CHAPTER 4

TWO APACHE WARRIORS

HEIR NAMES WERE Mangas Coloradas and Cochise. Both were warrior chieftains. They led the Apache people in more than a quarter century of brutal warfare with the young United States.

THE BACKGROUND OF A WAR

The ancestors of the Apache first lived in what is today's western Canada. At some point in the distant past, they migrated to the American Southwest, settling in the future states of Arizona, New Mexico, and Texas, while others made their homes in northern Mexico. They settled themselves in small groups that were eventually named for the areas in which they lived—Chiricahua Apache, Mescalero Apache, and Jicarilla Apache, to name just three.

The Apache called themselves Diné, meaning "the people." The name *Apache,* which translates as "enemy" in English, was given them by the Zuni Indians.

It was a fitting name. Though the newcomers were hunters of wild game and gatherers of plants, they were soon famous and hated as raiders. They attacked everyone around them and made off with everything needed for their survival—from pots, pans, and blankets to arms and livestock. No one was spared. Not their Indian neighbors—the Zuni, Hopi, and Pueblo among them. Not the

Spanish, who had invaded the Apache lands in the early 1500s and had governed the tribesmen harshly ever since, often taking them prisoner and putting them to work as slaves. And not the Anglo-Europeans who came streaming into the Southwest in the 1800s. Riding fast ponies, the Apache attacked villages, farms, ranches, and wagon trains, grabbed whatever they needed or wanted, and vanished as fast as they had come.

Between 1846 and 1848, however, the Apache and the Americans set aside the memories of the thefts and became allies. This sudden change took place when the United States declared war on Mexico. The Americans dreamed of spreading their nation out to the Pacific coast, and the Apache hoped to be free from years of a hated rule. The conflict that followed, the Mexican War, ended in a U.S. victory and the acquisition of millions of Mexican acres that would eventually become the states of California, Nevada, Arizona, New Mexico, Colorado, and Utah. They followed Texas into the Union. It had become a state in 1846.

The war put an end to Mexican rule of the Apache, but it saddled the tribe with a new problem. The Indians had thought that the U.S. government would order the Mexican population out of the region. They were quickly proved wrong. Not only did the Mexicans remain, but they were joined by a host of new whites who soon came flooding into the area—settlers, ranchers, businessmen, and adventurers of every stripe. They began shoving the Apache and neighboring tribes aside in the quest for any profit that might be won.

MANGAS COLORADAS

Though disappointed by these developments, the Apache remained at peace with the whites throughout the 1850s. Greatly responsible for the quiet was Mangas Coloradas, a chief of the Mimbres Apache, who lived in what would one day be southern New Mexico and Arizona. He kept the peace because he recognized the growing strength of the arriving Americans and how it was backed by a frontier army. The Mexicans, however, remained his traditional enemies and he constantly raided their villages and ranches.

But the chief's peaceful relations with the Americans came to a savage end in 1861. At that time, white miners were tunneling for gold near present-day Silver City in New Mexico. Their quest alarmed Mangas Coloradas on two counts: first, the whites were digging up a metal that was a symbol of the sun and thus sacred to the Apache; second, the chief feared that the tunneling might trigger devastating earthquakes.

Consequently, Mangas Coloradas paid several visits to the white mining camp and tried to talk the Americans into leaving. He told them of great gold deposits to the south in Mexico and volunteered to lead them there. The miners doubted his words and suspected that he intended to lure them into the desert and then kill them. Their suspicions drove them to a rash act that triggered twenty-five years of war by Mangas and his people.

When the chief next visited their camp, the miners suddenly grabbed him, wrestled him into submission, and tied him to a tree—no mean feat because Mangas, though in his sixties, was still a powerfully built man, standing 6 feet 4 inches (193 centimeters) tall and weighing at least 250 pounds (114 kilograms). They then lashed him mercilessly with a bullwhip, coming close to killing him.

As agonizing as his wounds were, they were nothing compared to the anger and degradation that Mangas felt. Such a beating as he had suffered ranked as one of the greatest insults an Indian could endure. In the weeks of his recovery, he nursed a growing hatred for the whites in his midst. Then, when healed, he laid siege to the gold camp where he had been so humiliated.

There, Mangas was joined by another great Apache, a warrior whose name had been Cheis, meaning "oak" in English, but had been expanded to "Cochise" by the whites. He was a chief of the Chiricahua branch in the future southeastern Arizona. The date of his birth was unknown but he was thought to be at least twenty years younger than Mangas. He was related to Mangas by marriage. His wife was the older chief's daughter.

COCHISE

In three ways, Cochise was much like Mangas. First, he was powerfully built, stood 5 feet 10 inches (178 centimeters) tall and weighed 175 pounds (79 kilograms). Second, in the wake of the Mexican War, he maintained peaceful relations with the growing white presence in his area, even while continuing the age-old Apache custom of attacking the surrounding Mexican farms and ranches for whatever booty they yielded. Finally, just as a cruel act by white miners had earned the hatred of Mangas Coloradas, so did a stupid act by a young army second lieutenant named George Bascom trigger Cochise's enduring rage and send him to war against the whites.

This abrupt change came at the beginning of 1861 when an Arizona rancher named John Ward brought frightening news to Bascom at a fort near the Arizona settlement of Tucson. Ward reported that a band of Indians had attacked his ranch and had made off with his adopted son and his herd of cattle. He accused Cochise of having led the attack.

Taking the rancher at his word, Bascom led some sixty men into the heart of Cochise country. At last, camping near a station owned by the Butterfield stage line, he sent a message to Cochise, requesting that the two of them meet. Thinking that the message was an offer of friendship,

Cochise rode into Bascom's camp in early February 1861. He brought with him his wife (the daughter of Mangas Coloradas, remember) and their two children, plus his brother and two nephews. They entered Bascom's tent and sat down to a meal and coffee with an officer who seemed to be a new white friend.

But, as soon as the dinner ended, Bascom became a changed man. He angrily accused Cochise of stealing Ward's cattle and child. Cochise denied the charge, insisted that he was innocent, and said that he would locate the guilty Indians and force the return of the cattle and child. Bascom stubbornly shook his head. Cochise and his party would be held prisoner until Ward's property was returned.

The outraged Cochise suddenly acted with blinding speed. All in one movement, he produced a knife, slashed open one wall in Bascom's tent, and plunged out into the night. He was met by a burst of gunfire from the startled sentries surrounding the tent, but Cochise managed to escape with a single bullet wound in his leg. In an hour he returned to a point a short distance from the camp and called out the request to see his brother. Bascom's reply was another burst of gunfire.

Cochise next tried to gain the release of his relatives by attacking the stagecoaches of the Butterfield line and offering the white passengers in trade. But all efforts to negotiate an exchange failed.

Mangas Coloradas and his Mimbres warriors, furious over Mangas's daughter's captivity, joined Cochise in the raids on local whites. On the opposite side of the fence, Bascom's troops captured three more Indians. Next, two army units battled the Apache down to the Mexican border. Before reaching the border and stepping beyond the reach of the army the Apache killed their prisoners. Bascom retaliated by hanging the Apache men he held. Cochise's wife and two children were later set free.

Army cavalrymen firing on Apache sheepherders in a canyon

The Apache immediately avenged the hangings. They swept through southeastern Arizona in a murderous rage. Left dead at their hands in a two-month killing spree were some 150 Mexicans.

THE CIVIL WAR YEARS

While Mangas Coloradas and Cochise were fighting together at the dawn of the 1860s, they noted a change in the Americans around them, soldiers and civilians alike. Both were vanishing from the Apache lands, a development that delighted the two men, Cochise in particular. He believed that the continuing Apache attacks were driving the whites away.

He was mistaken, as he would find years later. Behind the exodus was the Civil War. Troops from all points on the frontier were hurrying eastward to the battlefronts. Joining them were civilians of two types—those who planned to don either Union or Confederate uniforms, and those who feared that soon they would die at Indian hands now that there were no longer sufficient troops stationed nearby to protect them. In time, a few state militia volunteers took the place of the departed Union troops. The volunteers were soon running into arriving gray-uniformed Confederates. The two began to struggle for control of the frontier.

While it seemed a blessing to Mangas and Cochise, the disappearance of the regular army troops brought the two men to their next great battle. It was one that ended in defeat for both and another brush with death for Mangas.

The problem arose when the U.S. authorities in Washington, D.C., realized that the transfer of troops in the Southwest to the war front was leaving a freight and mail route that ran through Arizona to southern California unprotected from Indian attack. The same situation was being seen farther north along the highly traveled Oregon

TRIBES IN THE CIVIL WAR

Indian history repeated itself during the Civil War. As had happened decades earlier in the Revolutionary War, various Native American groups fought in the new conflict, with some supporting the North and others the South.

Though many, among them the Apache, did not take part, and used the departure of army units to the battlefronts as an opening for increased attacks on the whites in their midst, some 20,000 Indians did join the fighting, choosing one side or the other. They were to serve in Arkansas, Kansas, Missouri, North Carolina, Tennessee, and Texas.

A major share of the Native American involvement in the war, however, centered on the vast expanse of Indian Territory, which was located in today's state of Oklahoma. It began in 1861 when some Indians agreed to protect the region against a Confederate takeover. They were recruited by the Union Home Guard after the federal government dropped its policy against using Indian troops.

The Union was not alone in recruiting the Indians of the territory. The Confederacy also eagerly sought their help. It negotiated treaties that won the support of some leaders of the Territory's Five Civilized Tribes—the Cherokee, Chickasaw, Choctaw, Creek, and Seminole tribes. In the pacts, these leaders agreed to end their dealings with the United States and to raise regiments to help the South.

Other Indian nations living within Indian Territory took part in the war. Among them were the Caddo, Osage, and Wichita. Some fought for the Confederacy and some had divided their loyalties.

Beginning in 1862, Union forces made their way into Indian Territory. The invasion resulted in chaos for the Five Civilized Tribes. There had always been divisions within their ranks as to which side should be supported, and now the nations began to fight one another while simultaneously battling rebellions within their ranks.

It was fighting that ended in disaster for the Indians, no matter which side they supported. Left in ruins was the economy of Indian Territory. Even more tragic, the war had cost the Five Civilized Tribes approximately 6,000 lives out of a total population of 60,000.

Further, despite the fact that many members of the Five Civilized Tribes had fought for the Union, they were not protected by the federal government when peace returned. Washington, D.C., declared that its prewar treaties with the Five Civilized Tribes had been rendered void by the pacts with the Confederacy and forced the tribes to accept new agreements. The agree-

A June 1864 photograph shows General Ulysses S. Grant (standing, center) in camp with his aides. At far right is Lieutenant Colonel Ely S. Parker, a Seneca Indian.

ments required that they hand over the northern area of Indian Territory to the United States for white settlement.

The highest honors won during the war by Indians went to two men — Ely S. Parker and Stand Watie. Parker, a member of the Seneca nation, served as a captain with the Union forces and then, as a lieutenant colonel, worked as a secretary to General Ulysses S. Grant. When Grant later won the White House, he named Parker to the Board of Indian Commissioners.

Stand Watie, a Cherokee, served the Confederacy as an officer, rising to the rank of brigadier general. He was the only Indian, on either side, ever to achieve general rank.

and California trails. The army quickly dispatched two units of volunteer troops to guard the routes for the purpose of blocking a Confederate takeover of New Mexico.

On hearing that the unit assigned to the southern route had entered their territory, Mangas and Cochise decided to ambush and destroy it as it passed through the Chiricahua Mountains in the southwestern corner of Arizona. For the attack, they chose a place near an abandoned mail station called Apache Pass. They assembled more than one hundred of their braves there, positioning them behind rocks and bushes.

The ambush should have been an out-and-out defeat for the Americans when an advance party of 119 infantrymen and 7 cavalrymen entered the pass early in July 1862. But the loss finally went to the Apache. The Americans, in the midst of a storm of enemy bullets and arrows, managed to wheel two 12-pound (5-kilogram) howitzers into place. When their shells began exploding among the Apache, it sent the Indians fleeing.

The moment was a terrible one for the Apache. But a worse one came later in the day. The troop's supply wagons had been following several miles behind the advance group, and now six soldiers were sent galloping back to inform them of what had happened up ahead. A war party led by Mangas caught sight of the riders and swept down on them before they could reach their destination.

In the skirmish that followed, a trooper named John Teal crashed to the ground when his horse was felled by a bullet. He took shelter behind the animal's body and, certain that he was about to die, angrily promised himself to kill as many Apache as possible in his last moments. But he survived the attack when he took aim at a giant rider and felled Mangas Coloradas with a bullet to the chest. Immediately, the chief's companions dashed to his aid and carried him away, leaving Teal safely behind.

On departing the scene, the warriors crossed into Mexico and carried the wounded Mangas on a 120-mile (193-kilometer) ride to the tiny town of Janos. There, they hurried to the home of a Mexican doctor whose abilities, for some unrecorded reason, they admired more than those of their own healers. On the threat of killing everyone in town if he failed to remove the bullet successfully, they placed Mangas in his care.

Their faith was well placed. Mangas survived the surgery and returned to find Apache Pass and the land around it now firmly in U.S. hands. Though his wound was not yet fully healed, he set about raiding the surrounding towns, ranches, and military posts. In so doing, he earned the hatred of Brigadier General Joseph West, a new arrival as one of the military governors of the region. It was an enmity that drove West to decide that his problems with Mangas could be ended in just one way. The Indian had to be captured and killed.

West set about the capture by sending an officer to locate Mangas and invite him to visit a nearby army camp for talks leading to peace between the Indians and whites. Against the advice of friends who sensed treachery in the invitation, Mangas rode into the camp on January 17, 1863. Surprise and anger rushed through him in the next moments. Soldiers gripped his arms and told him that he was under arrest. He was then taken to a nearby fort. There, he was not placed in a cell but was given a blanket and told to sleep outdoors, next to a small campfire, while two troopers stood guard over him.

The story of what then happened was later told by a witness to the incident (a witness who has been variously reported as a sentry on duty nearby or a visitor to the fort). The witness said that he saw the two guards heat their bayonets in the campfire while Mangas slept. They then pressed the red-hot metal against Mangas's feet and legs.

When the Indian jerked upright in pain, the guards responded by swinging their rifles toward him and firing six shots into his body. Mangas died instantly.

West then reported to his superiors that the chief had been killed while attempting a nighttime escape. He conducted an "investigation" into the incident and cleared the two guards of any wrongdoing. All the while, it was widely known that the general had ordered the killing.

THE CIVIL WAR ENDS

With the death of Mangas, his fight was continued through the remaining Civil War years by his Mimbres, along with Cochise's Chiricahua and other groups. But the end of the Civil War brought the terrible realization that the outsiders were returning. Back to the Southwest came the troops that had vanished since 1861. With them came a new throng of white settlers. There was also the realization among the Indians that their cause was lost, no matter how valiantly they continued to fight. Their food supply was constantly low. Some of their finest warriors had been killed in the fighting. White attacks had decimated their villages and lost them too many lives.

A chance to end the conflict and rescue some of their ancient lands from white hands came soon after Ulysses S. Grant entered the White House in 1869 as the nation's eighteenth president. As one of his early official acts, the former head of the Union forces sent a commission to the Southwest with instructions to win a peace with the Apache and other Indians there and then to set aside reservations for their use. Named to head the commission were Brigadier General Oliver O. Howard and Vincent Colyer, a member of a Washington, D.C., agency that investigated reports of abuses against Indian groups.

His name in his native Chiricahua Apache was Goyathlay, meaning "one who yawns." The name by which he became known in U.S. history was Geronimo, given to him by his longtime enemies, the Mexicans. He was named for the saint known to the Spanish as San Geronimo, and to the English as Saint Jerome.

In 1850, when Geronimo was just twenty-one years old, the Mexicans won his enduring hatred by attacking his village and killing his wife and children. Retaliating throughout the next years, he so successfully avenged the deaths of his loved ones that the Mexicans—along with Americans and many Indians—began to credit him with supernatural powers. Awestruck, some insisted that he could not be wounded or killed by bullets.

In 1876, U.S. officials joined the Mexicans on his list of enemies when they forcibly moved his band of Chiricahua to the San Carlos Reservation, which stood on arid, unproductive land in eastern Arizona. Rather than submitting to the government-ordered move, Geronimo fled with a band of warriors and friends to Mexico. He then spent his time raiding settlements on both sides of the border, before being arrested a year later and returned to the reservation.

For the next few years, Geronimo divided his time between peacefully living on the reservation and breaking out for raids against the Mexicans and Americans. Then, in 1881, his life suddenly changed when American troops tried to arrest an Indian mystic named Nakaidoklini, who was prophesying that dead Apache warriors would soon return to rid the lands of the white intruders. The arrest attempt ended in the death of the prophet.

Enraged, Geronimo and a number of fellow Apache leaders began attacking the whites in the surrounding area, soldier and civilian alike, and then taking sanctuary in Mexico's Sierra Madre Mountains. With the consent of the Mexican authorities, U.S. troops went in search of the Indians, located them, and talked all the leaders into returning to the reservation, with Geronimo being the last one to arrive.

The commission established five agencies—one in New Mexico and four in Arizona—to work with the Apache and others in establishing reservations for them and providing them with needed supplies.

Of the Apache leaders who met with Howard, the most important was certainly Cochise. Tired of the endless

Apache leader Geronimo in 1887

He quickly became disgusted with reservation life and, in 1885, escaped across the border to the Sierra Madre with 150 followers. After being pursued by U.S. troops, he decided to return to Arizona the next year. He then escaped again, this time with over 20 supporters.

Once more, the U.S. Army went in pursuit of Geronimo, this time mustering five thousand soldiers for the job. Realizing that he was so outnumbered that this latest flight had no chance of success, the warrior surrendered in September 1886.

Contrary to the surrender agreement made with Geronimo, the U.S. government imprisoned the Apache leader and his followers in Florida until 1894. The group was then transferred to a prison in Oklahoma for several years. When finally set free, Geronimo worked as a rancher until his death in 1909. In the interim, he appeared in the Louisiana Purchase Exposition at St. Louis, Missouri, in 1905, and the next year rode in President Theodore Roosevelt's inaugural parade.

fighting, saddened at the suffering of his people, and exhausted from a burning stomach pain that kept him from taking food for long days at a time, Cochise met with Howard in 1872 and agreed to accept reservation life. But he did so only after Howard, at the end of seven days of negotiations, agreed that the reservation would be placed on the longtime Apache homeland encompassing Apache Pass.

In return for Howard's cooperation, Cochise promised that his people would keep peace on the reservation. It was a promise that he honored until the close of his life in 1874.

By the year of the warrior's death, almost all the Apache living in the Southwest had settled on reservations assigned to them in Arizona and New Mexico. Of those who so hated reservation life that they openly rebelled against it, the one who would be most widely remembered was Geronimo. He and his followers struggled in the white grasp for ten years, finally bringing the decades-long Apache war to a close with their surrender in 1886.

By that time, a decade had passed since one of the most famous battles in U.S. history—the deadly collision of American soldier and Native American warrior along the Little Bighorn River—had been fought.

CHAPTER 5

THE BATTLE OF THE LITTLE BIGHORN

THE EVENTS THAT LED TO the Battle of the Little Bighorn River on June 25, 1876, began nine years earlier when the U.S. government established the Great Sioux Reservation. Named for one of the two groups that would be its principal occupants—the other being the Northern Cheyenne—it was an enormous tract that covered the western half of today's South Dakota and a portion of North Dakota. Embracing millions of acres, it ranged west from the Missouri River to the edge of Wyoming Territory.

The reservation was created by the Treaty of Fort Laramie, an 1868 pact that was signed by the Lakota Sioux and the U.S. government. By the terms of the agreement, the government promised the Lakota people and the Northern Cheyenne that it would keep the reservation safe from white intrusions.

The Lakota were one of three Sioux-speaking people, the others being the Dakota and Nakota. The Cheyenne were divided between two groups, the Northern and the Southern. The Sioux and Cheyenne all lived in America's Great Plains region.

On two counts, the Fort Laramie pact was rejected by many Sioux and Cheyenne. They had no desire to become reservation Indians and, in view of what had happened to other tribal agreements with the United States, they had

A photograph from 1891 shows Sioux Indians at Pine Ridge Reservation,
originally part of the Great Sioux Reservation.

no faith in the federal government's promise to keep their land free of outsiders.

Consequently, many of the Sioux and Cheyenne refused to live on the reservation. Led by Sioux chiefs Red Cloud and Sitting Bull, they moved to what were called the unceded lands. These lands, where tribal hunting and fishing would be permitted, lay immediately to the west of the reservation, around the Powder River in today's Wyoming and Montana.

Though disliked by many Native Americans, the Great Sioux Reservation caused little trouble for several years. But a problem arose in 1873 when representatives of the Northern Pacific Railroad asked the Sioux for permission to lay tracks for a transcontinental railroad across the reservation. When the tribal leaders replied no with a grim-faced shake of their heads, they were greeted with the sight of railroad crews arriving to survey a route for the tracks. Immediately, the Sioux set about resisting this white intrusion.

Next, in 1874, the army sent Lieutenant Colonel George Armstrong Custer and his 7th Cavalry into the Black Hills region of the reservation. Custer was ordered to survey the area for future government use and also to see if there was any truth to a rumor that was reaching the white world—that the Black Hills were shot through with gold.

Geologists traveling with Custer turned the rumor into fact when they stumbled on large gold deposits. As soon as the word of their find reached the outside world, the Black Hills were overrun by hundreds of miners and adventurers, all of them ignoring the army's efforts to halt and turn them back. The Sioux and Cheyenne, watching their land being trampled, believed that the United States was breaking its treaty with them. They had ample reason—beyond the conflict over railroad building—for their suspicions. In the post-Civil War years, as increasing numbers of whites were advancing westward, the federal government was openly helping them along. Everywhere, Washington was either ignoring its pacts banning the American settlement of Indian land or pressing for treaty revisions that would make room for the growing white presence. Now the same thing was happening to the Great Sioux Reservation.

Furious at what they saw as one more American betrayal, many of the reservation people slipped away and fled west to the "unceded" lands along the Powder River. There, they joined forces with Sitting Bull and other rebellious chiefs.

In 1875 the federal government tried to quiet the situation. It offered to buy or rent the Black Hills region from the Sioux. Both offers were flatly refused.

Frustrated, Washington decided on a high-handed move against all the runaways now living in the Powder River region. In December 1875 it ordered them to return to the Great Sioux Reservation by the end of January 1876. Should they ignore the order, the government would regard them as "hostiles." They would be hunted down, arrested, and returned to the reservation by force.

Only a few runaways responded to the call. Most did not even hear it because they were wintering in remote areas. Even if the summons had been heard, a great many would have ignored it. They would have thought it too dangerous to break camp before the spring thaw.

ON THE ROAD TO DISASTER

When the deadline passed with the appearance of just a few reservation-bound families, Washington took the final step along the road that would lead to the Battle of the Little Bighorn. Major General Philip Sheridan, commanding all Union forces in the region extending from Montana to Texas, received orders to track down the fugitives and force their return. He immediately sent three search columns into the Powder River area, with each entering the region from a different direction.

First, troops under General George Crook were to march up from the south. They would advance from Fort Fetterman on the North Platte River in today's Wyoming. Under Crook's command would be one thousand men, plus some three hundred friendly Crow and Shoshone workers and white civilians.

Colonel John Gibbon, commanding the second column, would enter from the west, marching in from Fort Ellis in Montana. He would lead a combined force of infantry and cavalry.

Finally, the third force, headed by Brigadier General Alfred H. Terry, was to move west from Fort Abraham Lincoln in present-day North Dakota. Marching as part of Terry's force would be Lieutenant Colonel George Custer and his 7th Cavalry, a unit boasting some seven hundred men.

The three outfits were on the move in the spring of 1876. By mid-June, General Crook's 1,400 men were advancing north along Rosebud Creek, which lay a few miles to the east of the Little Bighorn. Through long days of marching, Crook had scanned the horizon for some sign of an Indian presence—and had seen nothing. But now, with an unnerving suddenness, his wait was over. As his men sipped their morning coffee on June 17, they were struck by as many as 1,500 warriors riding under the Oglala Sioux chief, Crazy Horse. A furious battle was triggered, raging for six hours.

In the first of those hours, Crook ordered two cavalry charges that hurled the braves back for a time. Crazy Horse then unleashed his horsemen against the cavalry. Fighting hand to hand, the Sioux and Cheyenne began to force the Americans into a retreat, only to be stopped by a Crook countercharge. The braves took cover in a ravine and were harried by the Americans until the general recalled his forces.

At day's end, both sides withdrew their forces. Crazy Horse vanished into the dusk. General Crook, with his troops sustaining light casualties but badly shaken, swung about and returned south to Fort Fetterman. The battle would go down in history as a draw, with both sides claiming victory, though both had withdrawn from the field.

ADVANCING ON THE LITTLE BIGHORN

Some 50 miles (81 kilometers) to the north of the Rosebud Creek fight, the units under General Terry and Colonel Gibbon finally came together at the point where the Yellowstone River met the Powder River. Both men were unaware of Crook's retreat back to Fetterman, but they were quickly handed another piece of vital information. It was carried in by Major Marcus Reno, the officer serving as second-in-command of Custer's 7th Cavalry.

Reno had been scouting south ahead of General Terry's force and now reported sighting fresh hoofprints leading in the direction of the Little Bighorn River, which the Sioux called Greasy Grass. Both Terry and Gibbon correctly guessed that an Indian group had been on its way to make camp alongside the river. What the two men could not possibly realize was the enormity of the camp. Gathering there in defiance of the U.S. order to return to the Great Sioux Reservation were warriors from six groups, among them the Hunkpapa and Oglala Sioux, along with Cheyenne and Arapaho comrades. Their camp stretched for just under 2 miles (3 kilometers) along the riverbank and was made up of about one thousand lodges.

The exact number of people in the camp has never been known, but it has been estimated at approximately 7,000, with between 1,000 and 2,000 of that number being warriors (some estimates run as high as 2,500 warriors). Among the chiefs present were Sitting Bull, Crazy Horse, and Crow King of the Sioux, and Lame White Man of the Cheyenne. Altogether, the camp housed the greatest number of Native Americans ever collected in one spot.

Immediately, Terry developed a plan for attacking the camp and taking its people prisoner for the trek back to the Great Sioux Reservation. All troops—except Custer's 7th Cavalry—would strike from the north. Custer, however, would move to a position south of the camp. He would then be ready to attack and, at the same time, be able to cut off any enemy retreat southward in the face of the Terry and Gibbon assaults.

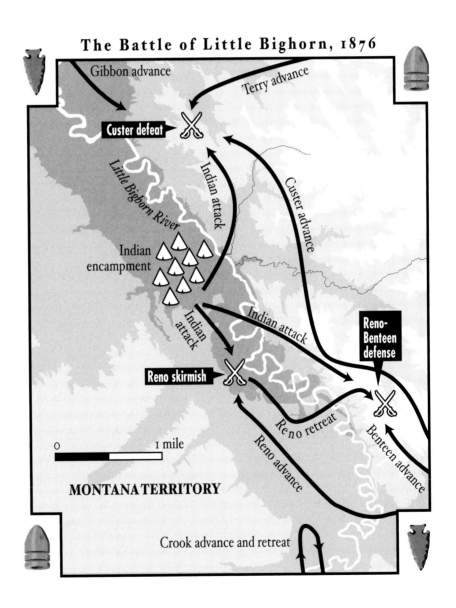

The Battle of Little Bighorn, 1876

General George A. Custer, photographed in the early 1860s

Son-of-the-Morning-Star was the name given to George Armstrong Custer by the Crow Indians, many of whom served as scouts with his 7th Cavalry. He was also known to the Indians as Long Haired Man.

Born in Ohio in December 1839, Custer was thirty-six years old when he lost his life at the Little Bighorn. He began his career by attending the military academy at West Point. Though graduating last in the class of 1861, he quickly proved himself to be a brilliant and fearless field officer in the Civil War. He was appointed to the staff of the Union commander, General George B. McClellan, and quickly rose to the honorary rank of major general at age twenty-five. En route, he earned a third nickname—The Boy General, bestowed on him by the Union press.

He married Elizabeth ("Libbie") Bacon during the war. When peace returned, his rank was returned to lieutenant colonel and he was given command of the 7th Cavalry. He led the 7th in battle against the Cheyenne in 1868 (see Chapter 3). Then, beginning in 1869, he served in several different western posts during what would be the final seven years of his life.

According to western legend, Custer once sat down with several Cheyenne leaders and shared a pipe signifying peace with them. He concluded the ceremony by solemnly saying that it was not his intention to make war against the Cheyenne ever again. The Cheyenne answered that, should he go back on his word at any time, he would die at Indian hands.

Once his cavalrymen were in place, Custer was to wait until June 27 before hitting the camp. By that time, Terry and Gibbon would be in place and ready to strike from the north. But Custer was also under orders to attack early if he considered it necessary. On Sunday, June 25, when his scouts reported sighting the camp, Custer quickly decided on an immediate attack. He thought that the Indians, on sighting his troops, might well try to flee.

It was a decision he reached without actually seeing the sprawling place for himself, because it was concealed behind rolling hills. Also without seeing for himself, he ignored the warnings of his Indian scouts that he would be hopelessly outnumbered. He shook his head when one scout bluntly told him that there were more warriors in the camp than his soldiers had bullets in their belts.

DEATH ON THE LITTLE BIGHORN

For the attack, Custer divided his command into four units. One consisted of his supply wagons; they were to remain in the rear until needed, while the other three struck the camp. He himself would lead one of the three attack groups. The other two would be headed by Major Reno and Captain Frederick Benteen. Reno and Benteen would lead a combined force of 400 men, with Benteen's unit being the smaller of the two. Riding with Custer himself would be some 230 men.

The three units were to advance northward along the east side of the Little Bighorn, with Benteen then to scout the hills southwest of the camp. At the same time, Reno was to strike the camp's southern end. Custer's plan for his own contingent has never been learned, but it is believed that he intended to continue up the east side of the Little Bighorn, swing about, and strike from the north.

Soon after they began to move, the day was marked with disaster for the Americans. First, at about 3:00 P.M., Reno found himself up against several hundred braves as he charged the southern end of the camp. A combined force of Sioux and Cheyenne came surging out to meet him. Intent on safeguarding their families, they hurled Reno back to a bluff overlooking the river. There, at 4:15 P.M., he was joined by Benteen's troops. The two units, fighting side by side, defended the bluff throughout the remainder of the day and then the next. Finally, the braves suddenly melted away. The two officers found that the disappearance was triggered by the arrival on the scene of General Terry and Colonel Gibbons.

Reno and Benteen reported that, of their combined force of approximately four hundred men, the fighting had cost them sixty wounded and just upward of fifty dead.

While Reno and Benteen were defending themselves, Custer and his men—five companies in all—continued north along the Little Bighorn. Suddenly, at about ten minutes after four that Sunday afternoon, a massive Indian force struck the troop.

Custer ordered his men to retreat and take up defensive positions along the crest of a ridge northeast of the encampment. It was there, in the midst of blinding clouds of dust and gunsmoke, that he and his men were overwhelmed by an estimated two thousand braves. The attackers swarmed over his defenses, driving arrows into the soldiers, snatching up the rifles of fallen cavalrymen and turning them on men still fighting, and themselves dropping when struck by riflemen sheltered behind fallen horses. By the time the fighting ended barely an hour later, the hillside was littered with bodies, Indian and white alike. All of Custer's troops—some 230 men—lay dead, with Custer's body sprawled among them.

Custer's Last Stand: The general and his soldiers are overrun by combined Indian forces at the Battle of the Little Bighorn, June 26, 1876.

When General Terry and Colonel Gibbons arrived at the battle site, they immediately visited the ridge where Custer and his men still lay. The two officers ordered that the bodies be buried near or on the spots where they had fallen. Removed earlier from along and below the ridge were the bodies of the fallen Sioux and Cheyenne. They had been carefully carried away by friends and relatives for burial elsewhere.

REVENGE

The news of what the press immediately called Custer's Last Stand reached the outside world in early July 1876, precipitating a wave of anger over the death of a soldier who had won national acclaim as a youthful Union general in the Civil War and as a dashing fighter against the Indians throughout the years since. In the next weeks, the nation's newspapers were filled with stories of how the army, infuriated and aching for revenge, began to track down all the Indians who had been at the Little Bighorn. The Indians had divided themselves into small groups and, still faced with the task of surviving, had returned to buffalo hunting. The next months produced the following actions:

September 7: Troops under General George Crook attacked a band of Dakota tribesmen at Slim Buttes, South Dakota, and imprisoned the few who had failed to escape to safety.

November 25: One of Crook's cavalry units attacked and overwhelmed a Cheyenne encampment on the Red Fork of the Powder River, killing forty warriors, burning their tepees, and destroying their food supplies.

January 1877: With General Nelson Miles in command, a force of some five hundred troops located and defeated Crazy Horse and his warriors in the battle of Wolf Mountain, Wyoming.

Added at later dates were such stories as these:

Chief Sitting Bull and his Hunkpapa followers took refuge in Saskatchewan, Canada, soon after Little Bighorn. When the supply of buffalo there dwindled, they returned to the United States in mid-1881 and surrendered to the authorities at Fort Buford in today's North Dakota. Sitting Bull spent the later years of his life on the Standing Rock Reservation in Dakota Territory.

Crazy Horse and his one thousand warriors fought the Americans until May 1877 when, freezing, they surrendered and were imprisoned at Fort Robinson, Nebraska. Four months later, Crazy Horse was fatally knifed in the back while trying to escape.

Though they were victorious on that June day in 1876, the battle of the Little Bighorn marked the beginning of the end for the Native Americans in their wars to protect their lands and preserve their ancient way of life. The wars would end on the eve of the twentieth century with the murder of Sitting Bull, followed by the massacre at Wounded Knee in today's South Dakota. In the years between, the people of the Nez Perce would stage one of the greatest flights to freedom in the nation's history.

CHAPTER 6

THE MAGNIFICENT MARCH

HE YEAR WAS 1855. As was reported in Chapter Three, Governor Isaac Stevens of Washington Territory called several local tribes to a conference at the settlement of Walla Walla. Among them were the Nez Perce. The tribesmen were famous as breeders of the Appaloosa horses and had lived in peace with the white man since meeting the Lewis and Clark Expedition back in 1805.

The name *Nez Perce,* meaning "pierced nose," had been given to them that same year by French traders on seeing that many decorated their noses with shells. The name by which the tribal members knew themselves was "Nee Mee Poo."

The Nez Perce did not realize it, but the conference with Stevens would mark the beginning of a tragic change in their lives. It would lead in some two decades to the loss of much of their land and mark the end of their era of peaceful coexistence with the white man.

Why? Because, in recent years, the American Northwest had been attracting a growing number of white settlers, so many that Governor Stevens now wanted to open the Indian lands to the newcomers for settlement, mining, and farming.

If the tribes at the conference accepted his plan, Stevens promised that the U.S. government would set aside acreage for their use alone and reward them with such benefits as homes, food, schools for their children, and grants of money. Reserved for the Nez Perce would be 10,000 square miles (26,000 square kilometers) in the region where the future states of Washington, Oregon, and Idaho would eventually meet. There, the Nez Perce lived in villages of fewer than seventy-five people each. It was land that they had long occupied and that included their cherished Wallowa Valley in Oregon. The valley was sacred to them as the home of their ancestors.

A treaty with the U.S. government resulted when many of the people agreed to the plan. But trouble came eight years later, in 1863, after a short-lived gold rush had brought a wave of prospectors flooding over the Nez Perce land. When many of the newcomers then stayed on through the years, the territorial officials met with the tribe for another conference. There, they proposed a new pact—one that would open the region wide to the whites by slashing the Nez Perce reservation from its present 10,000 square miles (26,000 square kilometers) to a mere 1,000 square miles (2,600 square kilometers), all of it across the border in Idaho Territory. Lost by the cut would be the entire Wallowa Valley.

Many Nez Perce vehemently opposed a plan that took away so much of their land and threatened the loss of the valley of their ancestors. Despite the opposition, however, a number of tribal chiefs approved and signed the new treaty. They did so out of fear that a rejection would drive the United States to war to get what it wanted. It would be a war that the Nez Perce could not possibly win. They had neither the money nor the manpower for victory.

There were several chiefs, however, who refused to sign the pact. Among them was the aged and respected Old Joseph, whose people lived in the Wallowa Valley. He had long been a friend of the settlers, but now he turned against them in anger. Defiantly, he and his followers continued to live in their beloved valley, resisting every U.S. attempt to oust them. Old Joseph died in 1871, with trouble erupting soon after.

NEW TROUBLE AND A NEW LEADER

It came with a wave of fresh settlers. On entering the valley, they recognized it as prime grazing land, claimed a portion of it for themselves, and established ranches there. But they were soon facing a new and determined Nez Perce chief—Young Joseph, the son of Old Joseph. A man in his early thirties, Young Joseph now quickly took action against the white invasion. He lodged a protest with the local Indian agent, a protest that eventually caused President Ulysses S. Grant to return the Wallowa land to the Nez Perce.

Grant's declaration, however, went ignored by the settlers. They continued to pour into the valley and even threatened death to any Nez Perce who got in their way. Their anger and their political power forced the president to change his mind. In 1875 he declared the Wallowa again open to white settlement. Then, in May 1877 the U.S. government ordered the Nez Perce to leave the valley and move to the land that had been reserved for them over in Idaho Territory.

The order was issued by General Oliver Howard, who was headquartered at the village of Lapwai inside the Idaho reservation. He told the valley people that they must be on their way to Idaho with all their livestock and belongings in thirty days. The United States would look on any failure to obey as an act of war.

The threat of a war infuriated the militant among Joseph's people, and many followers of other leaders. They wanted to fight, but Joseph argued that the order must be obeyed. The Nez Perce were courageous, but they had to remember that they did not have the strength for a war with the government. Reluctantly, the Nez Perce nodded and prepared for the hated move.

Then, suddenly, a new problem loomed for Joseph. It centered on Wahlitits, a young Nez Perce whose father had been murdered by a white settler named Larry Ott. At his father's dying request, the boy had never avenged the killing. But now, on being unfairly accused of cowardice by fellow tribesmen, he went looking for Ott, taking with him two friends.

The trio could not find their prey. Instead, they attacked four whites who were known for their hatred of all Indians. The attack, which left three of the whites dead, set off a killing spree by other young braves. At least fifteen more whites died in the next two days.

The killings brought the very real possibility of a war and led to a sudden flight by many Nez Perce. Certain that the U.S. Army would avenge the American deaths by loosing troops from their headquarters inside the new reservation, the Indians quickly headed for Idaho's White Bird Canyon. There, they could protect themselves if the pursuing soldiers wanted a fight. Also, there, they could talk peace if that was what the Americans wanted.

The move forced Joseph to a terrible decision. Should he join his people? Or should he avoid trouble? He decided on the first choice, but he insisted that his rebellious tribesmen honor two conditions of civilized conduct at all times. He would join and lead them only if they promised not to scalp anyone and not to kill women, children, and the wounded. When his conditions were accepted, he took his wife and infant daughter to White Bird Canyon.

With that step, he joined what would become one of the heroic flights for freedom in American history.

The Flight of the Nez Perce, 1877

Area of Detail

CANADA

MONTANA TERRITORY

WASH.
TERR.

Columbia R.

Bear Paw, (Sept-Oct)

Missouri R.

Cow Island (Sept)

Nez Perce
Reservation   Lolo Pass

Fort Missoula   Fort Shaw

Gen. Howard in pursuit

Route of Gen. Miles

Walla
Walla

Helena

Fort Keogh

Lapwai

Clearwater River
(July)

Snake R.

Yellowstone R.

Big Hole Valley (Aug)

Route of Col. Sturgis

Wallowa
Valley

Salmon R.

White Bird
Canyon
(June)

Bozeman   Fort Ellis

Canyon Creek (Sept)

Bighorn R.

Powder R.

ORE.

IDAHO TERRITORY

Camas Meadows (Aug)

Yellowstone National Park

WYOMING TERRITORY

Snake R.

0   100 miles

— Route of the Nez Perce
--- Route of the US Army
⬟ US Fort
✕ Battle

THE FLIGHT: THE FIRST BATTLES

While the Nez Perce were gathering at White Bird
Canyon, General Howard sent a force of one hundred cavalrymen to locate their camp, a search that finally led to the
canyon in mid-June. The tribal leaders, hoping that the
chance was at hand for a talk with the Americans, sent a
party of six under a flag of truce to meet the soldiers. But
all chances for a peaceful talk ended when a rifle was fired
at the Indians' approach. The bullet sang harmlessly past

them, but caused an immediate return fire. Two army buglers pitched from their saddles, dying instantly. (To this day, no one knows who fired the original shot, but it has been long agreed that a trooper was likely at fault.)

What followed was a blood-soaked defeat for the soldiers. Firing from behind great boulders, the Nez Perce drove the blue-coated troopers back and sent them galloping off to their fort, wounding four and killing thirty-eight

General Oliver Howard pursues fleeing Nez Perce on Dead Mule Trail, Idaho, in 1877.

in the process. Even better, the Americans left behind a supply of new rifles at White Bird Canyon, all of them sorely needed by the Indians.

Though proud of the victory, the Nez Perce realized that they could not remain in the area. Howard would surely send a larger force to take revenge for the U.S. humiliation, and then herd the Indians onto their new reservation. The Indians were right. Within a few days, Howard was on the march with several hundred men. But so was Joseph. Leading some 650 people, some of whom were not Nez Perce, he abandoned the canyon.

For a month the Nez Perce evaded Howard's troops. During that time, a contingent of the colonel's men, seemingly for no reason, attacked a village occupied by the people of Chief Young Looking Glass. Young Looking Glass had always avoided trouble with the whites, but his attitude was now abruptly changed. He and his people joined Joseph in flight.

With the arrival of Looking Glass and his followers, the Nez Perce ranks grew to approximately eight hundred. But Joseph could only shake his head sadly. Of that total, some five hundred were women, children, and men too old for fighting. A mere three hundred were braves.

But they were a magnificent three hundred. On July 11, 1877, when the tribe was camped alongside the Clearwater River, they had to face a sudden attack by Howard. They fought the enemy to a standstill for two days, enabling their loved ones to flee to safety before escaping themselves. Howard limped off with thirteen dead and forty wounded. The Nez Perce suffered just four wounded and six dead.

Soon after the Clearwater triumph, Joseph's fellow chiefs summoned him to a meeting. Among those in attendance were Ollikut (who was Joseph's brother), Lean Elk, Toohoolhoolzote, Rainbow, Five Wounds, and the newly arrived Looking Glass. Until then, the Indians had fought to keep the Americans at a distance. But now it was time for them to decide on a plan that would determine the course of their lives for all time to come.

In a long debate, Joseph argued that the tribe should return to the Wallowa Valley and fight to reclaim their land. But Looking Glass shook his head. The Nez Perce, he said, were pitted against too many Americans to risk a war. It was a war they had no chance of winning.

Looking Glass urged the chiefs to lead the people out of the region. Let them cross the Bitterroot Mountains to their east, he argued, and then drop into Montana Territory. There, they would find plenty of buffalo. There, they could befriend the Crow tribe. There, they could build a new life, free of the Americans. The Americans would leave them alone, glad to see them gone.

Joseph objected, but to no avail. Then, since Looking Glass was responsible for voicing the plan, the chiefs named him to lead the march to a new life. Joseph, despite his opposition, now gave his support to Looking Glass.

THE FLIGHT: THE LONG MARCH

The march to a new life took the Nez Perce through the Bitterroot Mountains and into Montana. They cut southwest to give Howard a wide berth, only to have scouts bring word that troops from nearby Fort Missoula had built a temporary fort up ahead. On July 25 the Indians bypassed the crude installation by working their way along a mountain slope. Then they marched south to the Big Hole Valley.

There, Looking Glass ordered a stop for a much-needed rest. He could see that everyone was exhausted and on the brink of starvation. But, though recognizing that he was right, some of the chiefs objected to the stop, saying that it would give the pursuing troops the chance to catch up and attack. Looking Glass shook his head. He believed that his people had evaded Howard and had left him far behind. They could rest here safely for a time before the final march to a meeting with the Crow.

It was a tragic decision. Howard was still close on their heels. Through a constant exchange of telegraph messages with the U.S. forts in the area, he knew exactly where the Nez Perce were when they finally stopped in the Big Hole Valley. It was there that a contingent of some two hundred troopers finally caught up with them at sunrise on August 9, 1877.

The fighting began when one of the Nez Perce chiefs came out of his tepee and, astonished, caught sight of blue-jacketed figures crawling through the surrounding underbrush. He sounded the alarm and then fought the soldiers for a few scant minutes before dying of bullet wounds. His son rushed out to meet the attack, armed only with a bow and arrow. He fell when struck by a bullet.

In mere minutes, the attack turned the camp into a blazing inferno. Rising and firing pistols and rifles as they ran, the Americans charged among the tepees dotting the camp and set them afire. Making no distinction among men, women, and children, they opened fire on anyone who loomed in front of them. By the time the attack ended, eighty-nine Indians lay dead. Of that number, seventy-seven were women, children, and elderly males. Twelve were warriors.

Though badly beaten, the Indians counterattacked the next day. They drove the Americans back and held them at bay while the surviving women, children, and the elderly escaped into the distance. When their people were safely away, the braves abandoned the fight, rejoined the tribe, and hurried southeast. Left behind were sixty-nine army casualties—thirty dead and thirty-nine wounded.

A STRANGE MOMENT AT YELLOWSTONE

In the wake of their attack on the Camas Meadows encampment, the Nez Perce entered the northwest corner of Wyoming Territory. There, advancing quietly, some on foot and some on horseback, they surprised large groups of Americans amid the splendors of the surrounding scenery.

The astonished Americans were on vacation that August of 1877, visiting Yellowstone National Park, enjoying its natural beauties, and now staring at an unexpected sight—a sight that left no doubt of how greatly the United States was changing. The Nez Perce were saying farewell to their land as they had always known it, while the Americans were visiting a once wild area that had now become the country's first national park.

Yellowstone had been designated as a national park just five years earlier, in 1872. Covering 3,468 square miles (9,017 square kilometers), the park today spreads through southern Montana, eastern Idaho, and northwestern Wyoming.

The Nez Perce deaths at Big Hole Valley brought a change in the Indian leadership. The tribe lost faith in Looking Glass and replaced him with Chief Lean Elk. Lean Elk then led the way southeast toward Wyoming Territory, pausing a few miles from the border to drive off two hundred pack animals from a U.S. encampment at Camas Meadows. The travelers then passed through Yellowstone National Park and reentered Montana.

There, their hopes of starting life anew with the Crow were swiftly dashed. The Crow leaders greeted them coldly and said that the tribe was not interested in an alliance of any sort. They wanted no part of the renegade Nez Perce, certain that an alliance would bring the wrath of the U.S. government down on their heads.

Stunned by this unexpected setback, the Nez Perce chiefs met to discuss their next move. The decision: March north, leave the United States, and enter Canada. There, they would find the great Sioux warrior Sitting Bull, who had fled to Canada with his followers in the wake of Little Bighorn. Surely he would come to the aid of fellow sufferers. The tribe, now battered and beginning to starve, set out for Canada.

The trek north to the border was marked by trouble from its beginning. First, a new enemy galloped into view—a 350-man troop, under Colonel Samuel Sturgis from Fort Keogh in eastern Montana. The newcomers caught sight of the Nez Perce on September 13 and attacked along a dry streambed called Canyon Creek. In a stubborn defensive action, the Indians held the enemy at bay while their families escaped to safety and then, while making an orderly retreat, slowed the American pursuit by blocking their path with boulders and brushwood. The Americans finally gave up the chase and, low on rations, abandoned the campaign.

Though victorious, the Nez Perce were exhausted and starving as they struggled north in the next days. Their march was marked constantly by tragedy. Their horses began to drop with exhaustion. The children grew weak and skeletal with hunger. The aged fell daily, either too tired to walk another step or to rise from their blankets at dawn. They had to be left behind, along with braves whose battle wounds finally made further travel impossible.

The tribe reached Cow Island in far northern Montana on September 23. From there, they pushed north, past the Bear Paw Mountains, at last sighing with relief when they put the mountains behind them and made camp alongside Snake Creek at month's end. Finally, after weeks of travel, they felt safe. The Canadian border was now about 40 miles (64 kilometers) away. Surely, they had left their pursuers far behind. They could now rest a little before marching the final miles to their new home.

They were tragically wrong.

The Nez Perce did not know it, but the army was snapping at their heels. Riding in pursuit were two units—first, General Howard's soldiers, and second, a combined cavalry and infantry force of four hundred under General Nelson Miles. The Miles unit was stationed at Fort Keogh, which was located some 200 miles (322 kilometers) to the southeast of the Bear Paw range. On the basis of telegraph messages from Howard, General Miles was plunging forward along a line that would enable him to intercept his Indian prey a few miles south of the Canadian border.

Miles sighted the Indian camp at dawn on September 30. He immediately ordered a series of attacks, only to see each one falter in the face of a stubborn resistance. Meeting his cavalry and infantry were the last of the Nez Perce warriors, side by side with the remnants of the tribe's women, children, and aged. While the warriors shredded the blue-coated ranks with rifle fire, everyone else fought with rocks, sticks, and cooking knives. Miles finally called off the attack.

The rattle of gunfire was now replaced by the rumble of artillery pieces rolling into place opposite the Nez Perce camp. Then came their thunder, marking the opening of a siege that would last until Miles raised a white flag and offered the chance for the Nez Perce to talk peace.

By that time, all but one of the Nez Perce leaders had fled into Canada or had died, among them Looking Glass and Lean Elk. Only Chief Joseph remained to speak for the surviving Nez Perce—some 350 women and children and 80 men, all of them starving and chilled to the bone with the first snows of the year.

Miles raised the white flag on October 1. He and Joseph then met at a point midway between the opposing

Chief Joseph of the Nez Perce

lines for a talk that led nowhere. Miles wanted a complete surrender, one that would require the Indians to lay down all their weapons. Joseph shook his head. His people must keep half their arms. They would be needed for hunting and self-protection.

The talks continued for several days, covering various issues but reaching no firm agreements. Then, on October

4, General Howard arrived on the scene. He immediately sent a simple message to Joseph: Miles and he were tired of the war and wanted to be done with it. Knowing that the fighting could now be ended quickly, Joseph agreed to meet with the two officers at sunset.

The chief felt a deep sense of relief. He believed that he was now achieving a peace with pride and honor. His people had not been captured or defeated. The fighting was ending in a draw. Further, based on his talks with Miles, Joseph believed he was participating in a conditional surrender, meaning that his people would not be punished for their fight and would be allowed to return to their Idaho homeland to live on their reservation there.

At sundown Joseph mounted his pony. Followed by several of his finest warriors, he rode slowly to the U.S. lines. Waiting there were Howard and Miles, with ranks of blue-coated troops standing at attention behind them. Howard, though he was the superior officer, gave Miles, the man who had done the fighting, the honor of accepting the Indian surrender.

Joseph, speaking while a translator turned his words into English, described his reasons for ending the fighting. Historians today believe that Joseph did not actually speak the following words, but that they were given their eloquent expression by the translator:

> I am tired of fighting. Our chiefs are killed . . . The old men are all dead . . . It is cold and we have no blankets. The little children are freezing to death. My people, some of them, have run away to the hills and have no blankets, no food. No one knows where they are—perhaps freezing to death. I want to have time to look for my children and see how many I can find. . . .

Then Joseph spoke the words that were to echo through the years and earn him a lasting place in American history:

LIFE AFTER THE FIGHTING

Though his flight won Joseph the admiration of Americans everywhere, he was forced to suffer another insult from the United States immediately following his surrender. Though General Miles promised that he could return to his beloved Wallowa Valley in the spring of 1878, the federal government ignored that promise, shipping Joseph and certain of his followers to Kansas instead. They were then moved to Indian Territory for several years.

In the mid-1880s, Joseph's followers were allowed to return to the Wallowa Reservation. But not their chief. Beginning in 1888, he was imprisoned on the Colville Reservation in today's Washington. Except for a brief visit just before his death, he was not permitted ever to see his beloved homeland.

Joseph died in 1904. His exact age was unknown, but he was thought to be in his mid-sixties. On the chief's death, the reservation doctor who attended him in his final days simply wrote: "Joseph died of a broken heart."

Hear me, my chiefs. I am tired. My heart is sick and sad. From where the sun now stands, I will fight no more forever. . . .

The long march had taken four months and had covered an exhausting 1,700 miles (2,737 kilometers). The strength and courage that it had required of Joseph and his people would win them the nation's undying admiration.

CHAPTER 7

DEATH AT WOUNDED KNEE

THE BATTLE OF THE LITTLE BIGHORN in 1876 and the valiant march of the Nez Perce to freedom the next year were the last great actions in the American Indian Wars. Slowly, realizing that the white settlers' advance westward would never be turned back, the tribes surrendered their lands and allowed themselves to be placed on reservations, there to live a life alien to their cultures. Their days of warfare were at an end, except for outbreaks here and there.

1878: The Cheyenne
On being tracked down by army troops, the Northern Cheyenne who had fought at Little Bighorn were banished to Indian Territory. Hating life there, 297 of their number—men, women, and children—stole away in September 1878. They broke into two groups and eluded the army's every effort to capture them as they began fleeing to their old homeland in Wyoming and Montana. One group—made up of the tribe's old and sick—was finally caught when stalled in an October blizzard. The group spent the winter imprisoned at a fort and then escaped for a time, with most of their number then losing their lives in a vicious army roundup. Later, the Cheyenne were allowed to settle in their Wyoming and Montana homeland.

1878: The Bannock and Paiute

Fighting exploded this year when the Bannock and Paiute tribes of Oregon and Idaho finally lost their tempers over how the camas root, a staple of their diet, was being destroyed by hogs belonging to the surrounding white ranchers. Their anger led to a war in which two hundred Bannocks and Paiutes clashed with a group of white volunteer militia. Regular army troops then moved in and pursued the Indians through parts of Oregon and Idaho. The chase ended in autumn with the capture of about five hundred Indians.

1879: The Utes

This year, the Utes in Colorado reacted in fury to the damage done to their reservation lands by invading whites who were searching for the lead deposits that had been found there a year earlier. The uprising featured a weeklong siege of an army wagon train that took the lives of nine white settlers and fourteen soldiers. The siege ended when the Ute chief, Ouray, called a halt to the fighting.

Though the Native American defense of their lands throughout the United States was over by the late nineteenth century, one more tragedy of death for the Indians—and tragedy of shame for the whites—remained. It was the tragedy of Wounded Knee Creek in 1890.

THE GHOST DANCERS

By the dawn of the 1890s, the Sioux and their fellow tribes were living in desperate circumstances. The U.S. government had reduced the Great Sioux Reservation to half its size, freeing thousands of acres in the former Dakota Territory (since 1889, the states of North and South Dakota) for white settlement. The remaining Great Sioux land was divided into six small reservations—Cheyenne River, Crow Creek, Lower Brule, Pine Ridge, Rosebud, and Standing Rock.

The loss of so much land was humiliating for the Indians, as was the requirement that they forget their old ways and learn to live in the manner of the whites. Added to this hardship was the failure of the U.S. government to honor its promise of increased food shipments in exchange for their lost lands.

It was a time when the Lakota Sioux felt the desperate need for some sign of hope for the future. They suddenly found it in what became known as the Ghost Dance Religion. Founded in the Nevada of the late 1880s by a Paiute religious leader named Wovoka, it held out the promise that the world and the hated white man would soon perish, with the earth then returning to life and bringing with it the giant buffalo herds of old and all the Native American ancestors who had died since the dawn of time.

To make this miracle possible, Wovoka said that the Indians must sing certain songs and dance to them. In the dances—known collectively as the Ghost Dance—the participants might die for a few moments and be allowed to see what paradise held for them one day. Further, they must daily live in harmony with all of nature, be honorable in their every dealing, keep their bodies cleansed, and shun the ways of the whites. In particular they were to avoid the white use of alcohol.

The Ghost Dance Religion and its beliefs spread widely in just a few months and was brought to the Lakota Sioux by two medicine men—Kicking Bear and Short Bull—who had visited with Wovoka. However, the kind of religion preached by the two men differed much from Wovoka's. They called for the people to ignore his peaceful intent and, according to a reservation agent who had heard their words, to seek the death of all whites. Further, they urged their fellow tribesmen to face the whites fearlessly, saying that there were special Ghost Dance shirts that would make their wearers safe from enemy harms. The fervor that gripped the reservation people quickly put the U.S. offi-cials in charge there on their guard. Out went an order that the Ghost Dances were to be stopped immediately—an order that was just as immediately ignored.

THE STEPS TO WOUNDED KNEE

When the Ghost Dancing continued, a new order was issued, this one summoning army troops to the Rosebud and Pine Ridge reservations, where the phenomenon seemed to be at its most popular. Leading the troops was General Nelson Miles, who had so successfully pursued and fought the Sioux in the wake of Little Bighorn.

Kicking Bear and Short Bull, now wanted for bringing the Ghost Dance to the Sioux, immediately fled, taking their followers to a spot in a remote corner of the Pine Ridge Reservation. On their arrival, they sent a message to Sitting Bull, inviting him to join them. The chief, living on the Standing Rock Reservation, accepted the invitation, though he had his doubts about the validity of the Ghost Dance beliefs. He only permitted the dance because he believed his people desperately needed a renewed sense of strength and destiny.

But word of the invitation reached U.S. government ears before Sitting Bull could depart for Pine Ridge. On orders from General Miles, the reservation police, a force manned by Indians, immediately attempted to arrest the chief. Their arrival at his cabin on December 15, 1890, ended moments later in an explosion of gunfire. In the stunned quiet that followed, Sitting Bull, shot twice, lay dead with seven of his warriors and six members of the police unit.

Sitting Bull's arrest was not the only one sought by Miles. The general also ordered that another chief—Big

Foot of the Lakota Sioux—be arrested for leaving his home on the Cheyenne River Reservation with a band of followers. Miles assumed that Big Foot planned to join the escaped Ghost Dancers. He was mistaken—an error that would soon end in tragedy. Big Foot was marching to Pine Ridge to urge that peace be restored there. Though he had once favored the Ghost Dance movement, he no longer supported it.

Miles immediately sent Custer's old outfit—the 7th Cavalry—in search of Big Foot. A detachment caught up with the Indian in late December, only to have him slip away in the night. He and his people then struggled through a heavy snowfall until a band of pursuing troops overtook them on December 28. By now, the Indians were short of food, starving, and freezing. Big Foot himself lay in a wagon, close to death with pneumonia.

When the troops arrived, the chief told their commander in a hoarse whisper that his people no longer had the strength to fight or flee. They were ready to surrender. The commander replied by ordering them to move 5 miles (8 kilometers) westward and make camp by Wounded Knee Creek. He would then escort them to the headquarters of the Pine Ridge Reservation, some 20 miles (32 kilometers) distant.

On reaching the creek, the Indians received food and tents from the troops and saw that they were in a shallow valley lying near a low rise called Cemetery Hill. Stationed on the flatland near the creek and up on Cemetery Hill were some five hundred soldiers. Four small-caliber cannons were ranged along the hilltop, their muzzles pointing at the Sioux shelters.

Three hundred fifty Indians were now camped with the desperately ill Big Foot in the midst of this armed might. Women and children made up over 200 of their number.

When December 29, 1890, dawned full of the threat of a snowfall, the Indian men were ordered to fetch all their weapons from the surrounding shelters and hand them over to the troops. When some of the men, fearful of being left unarmed, went at the task too slowly, the soldiers roughly pushed everyone aside and shouldered their way into the shelters, pawing at blankets, clothing, and cooking utensils, and cursing as they tossed out everything from knives to bows, arrows, and rifles.

Their roughness added to the nervousness and anger felt by the Sioux warriors. A shaman named Yellow Bird then worsened matters by losing his temper and demanding that the warriors put a stop to what was happening. Those who were wearing Ghost Dancer shirts, he shouted, could attack the soldiers in perfect safety.

Fortunately, Yellow Bird's demands went ignored. But more trouble—deadly trouble this time—came moments later when the soldiers decided to search the Indian men for weapons possibly hidden beneath the blankets draped around their shoulders. It was then that they encountered young Black Coyote. Perhaps not understanding all that was happening, because he was deaf, the boy struggled to keep his new rifle when a cavalryman tried to snatch it away. The morning air was shattered when the gun was accidentally discharged.

Many historians today believe that the story of Black Coyote may be no more than legend. They point out that no one knows what actually happened. But, no matter whether the story is fact or fiction, there was instant chaos everywhere. Army rifles began exploding, with much of the fire coming from the troops up on Cemetery Hill. Caught in the initial burst, many of the Sioux—men, women, and children—spun and pitched to the frozen ground. Men who were not hit tried to sprint to the weapons that had been taken from them. Some of the women ran screaming to the soldiers and began to beat them with their fists. Others snatched up their children and dashed to a shallow ravine that ran near the campsite. There, some threw the children to the ground and shielded them with their bodies. Others, clawing in the dirt at the side of the ravine, tried to dig holes in which to shelter the little ones. All the while, the soldiers up on Cemetery Hill fired down on the encampment while those below now dashed among the fallen Indians, thrusting their bayoneted rifles in all directions.

And, up on the hilltop, the four cannons opened fire, with their shells ripping apart tents and tepees. But then, as suddenly as it had started, the horror ended. It had lasted less than an hour, though it would continue for a number of Indians who fled from the camp and would be killed in the next hours by pursuing troops. Lying dead at Wounded Knee were at least 150 of Big Foot's people, among them the chief himself. Some 50 Sioux were wounded, with many of their number fated to die of their wounds in the next hours or days.

Of the more than 500 American troops that morning, 25 were dead and 39 wounded. Most of the casualties were victims of the gunfire of their comrades.

The terrible drama of Wounded Knee continued in the next weeks. The bodies of Big Foot and his people were placed in a community grave and covered over without ceremony. The fighting erupted afresh when a band of Sioux who had escaped the slaughter attacked a 7th Cavalry troop some miles to the north and left two soldiers dead and five wounded. Many Sioux continued to gather about Kicking Bear and Short Bull for a time, but soon returned to their normal lives as the Ghost Dance craze

Gathering up the frozen dead from the battlefield at Wounded Knee on January 1, 1891

began to fade. Among them was Wovoka, who finally recognized the futility of trying to stem the white tide. He was reported as calling upon his followers to travel a new trail:

"The only trail now open—the white man's trail."

EPILOGUE

JUST OVER A CENTURY HAS PASSED since the tragedy at Wounded Knee marked the end of the Indian Wars. Since then, there have been many changes in the lives of the nation's Native Americans.

At the time of Wounded Knee, there were an estimated 250,000 Native Americans in the United States, a frightening drop of 750,000 from the 1 million said to be living here before the arrival of outsiders with their wars, crimes, and diseases. Today, that great loss has been restored. The total U.S. Native and Alaskan Native populations currently stand at 2.5 million.

LIFE TODAY

About half the nation's Native Americans today live on some 550 federal reservations and 275 land areas that are administered as reservations. The reservations and areas vary in size from 100 acres (41 hectares) to 16 million acres (6.5 million hectares). The remaining half of the people resides in cities, towns, and rural areas throughout the country. They share with their fellow Americans of all ethnic backgrounds the same interests in home, family, politics, and entertainment. They eat the same food and wear the same clothing.

The same holds true for the work done by Indians. It matches that done by Americans everywhere and ranges from laboring jobs to the professions and the arts. Further, ever since the late 1980s, many tribal leaders have found a new way of providing employment and bettering the lot of their people. They have turned to legal gambling and, as a result, have created 125,000 jobs (not only for Native Americans but for all citizens) in reservation casinos, hotels, and restaurants, plus another 160,000 indirectly connected to gaming. Indian gambling is currently a $6-billion-a-year industry. Along with providing employment, its funds go toward the establishment of housing, public buildings, roads, health care, and education for the Indian population.

There was a time when only a few Native Americans were known to the general public for their accomplishments. Among them were athlete Jim Thorpe (a gold medal winner for track in the 1912 Olympic Games and, in 1963, a charter member of the Pro Football Hall of Fame) and Ira Hayes (who won fame in World War II as one of the soldiers who raised the American flag atop Mount Suribachi following the battle of Iwo Jima).

Today, however, the number who have won widespread recognition are many. They include actor Graham Greene for his work in motion pictures (*Dances With Wolves*) and television (the series "Northern Exposure"); writers N. Scott Momaday and Linda Hogan; singer Buffy Sainte-Marie; artist Harry Fonseca; and social activist Wilma Mankiller.

To prepare their young for future work and success, today's Native Americans maintain a number of their own elementary and high schools within the country's regular public school systems, plus more than thirty colleges. The courses of study are the same as in American schools everywhere, but with a heavy emphasis on curriculum about tribal ways, ceremonies, and languages, so that age-old customs and traditions will not be forgotten. Gone is the day when the teaching of tribal languages was banned in reservation schools.

TOWARD THE FUTURE

The Native American journey to the successes of today has been steadily accompanied by hardship. A chief example can be seen in the history of the Indian treaty. Between its birth in 1778 and its end in 1871, the treaty process resulted in some 370 pacts being ratified by the U.S. Senate, with 45 others successfully negotiated but then not ratified by Congress. Sadly, the federal government then violated the terms of all but a few. The violations were chiefly aimed at taking away tribal lands so that they could be opened for white development.

In addition, the early reservation system was rife with problems. The system showed little care for the dismal realities of reservation life. Hunger, inadequate medical care, poor housing, and the lack of proper educational facilities were (as some still continue to be) problems.

The system did nothing to ease the anger felt toward each other by both Indians and whites after decades of warfare and prejudice. The Indians thought of themselves as enslaved and ignored by the whites, while many whites regarded the Indians as idlers surviving on the largesse of the government.

In 1887, Congress sought to improve this situation with the General Allotment Act. Its purpose was to turn reservation Indians into farmers who would be able to support themselves and, in so doing, take a new pride in themselves and win the respect of the Americans. It would do this by awarding parcels of land of varying sizes within the reservations to the tribes.

But matters did not work out as planned. Many Native Americans had neither a taste nor a talent for farming. And not all the reservation land went to the Indians. There was leftover acreage—much of it extremely valuable—that ended up in government hands and was then placed on sale for non-Indian purchase, with the proceeds of the sales to be placed in trust for the Indian nations. The amounts of property that passed into white hands increased with the coming of the twentieth century. By 1934 tribal-owned lands had fallen to 52 million acres (21 million hectares). They had added up to 138 million acres (56 million hectares) in the late 1880s.

Ever since 1924, there has been an enlightened series of moves to reform the government's treatment of the Indian population. That year, Congress granted citizenship and the right to vote to the Native American. In a 1937 act, the federal government began to correct the many problems that started with the General Allotment Act; improved were the regulations governing the sale of reservation acreage and the return of land to Native American owner-ship. Also, steps were taken to improve living conditions on the reservations, to end bans against the practice of ancient religious ceremonies, and to permit the teaching of tribal languages in the schools.

But, despite the improvements, there remained—and still remain—problems needing to be solved, among them the lack of education, the poverty, and the disease yet found on some reservations. The 1960s and 1970s brought widespread activity by groups working for the improvement of Indian life everywhere, among them the National Indian Youth Council and the American Indian Movement. These organizations participated in a variety of public actions: the 1969 occupation of Alcatraz Island in San Francisco Bay, where the protesters claimed the right to possess the island under an 1868 treaty that gave surplus federal land to Indians; the 1972 march from San Francisco to Washington, D.C., on behalf of tribal treaty rights; and the 1973 occupation of the village of Wounded Knee for seventy-one days to protest the poor living conditions found in the surrounding reservations, chief among them the Pine Ridge Reservation.

The twentieth century was a critical one in the Native American—and government—efforts to overcome the problems that were born in the years of wars. There can be no doubt that the new century will see further progress in solving those problems that remain.

BIBLIOGRAPHY

Avery, Susan, and Linda Skinner. *Extraordinary American Indians.* Chicago: Children's Press, 1992.

Axelrod, Alan. *Chronicle of the Indian Wars From Colonial Times to Wounded Knee.* New York: Prentice Hall, 1993.

Axelrod, Alan, and Charles Phillips. *The Macmillan Dictionary of Military Biography.* New York: Macmillan, 1998.

Baldwin, Gordon C. *Indians of the Southwest.* New York: G. P. Putnam's Sons, 1970.

Bleeker, Sonia. *The Apache Indians: Raiders of the Southwest.* New York: William Morrow, 1951.

Brinkley, Douglas. *American Heritage History of the United States.* New York: Viking Penguin, 1998.

Brown, Dee. *Bury My Heart at Wounded Knee.* New York: Henry Holt, 1974.

Carnes, Mark C., John A. Garraty, and Patrick Williams. *Mapping America's Past: A Historical Atlas.* New York: Henry Holt, 1996.

Chambers, John Whiteclay II, ed. *The Oxford Companion to American Military History.* New York: Oxford University Press, 1999.

Dolan, Edward F. *Beyond the Frontier: The Story of the Trails West.* New York: Benchmark Books, 2000.

English, June A., and Thomas D. Jones. *Scholastic Encyclopedia of the United States at War.* New York: Scholastic, 1998.

Fleischner, Jennifer. *The Apaches: People of the Southwest.* Brookfield, Conn.: The Millbrook Press, 1994.

Hirschfelder, Arlene. *Native Americans: A History in Pictures.* New York: Dorling Kindersley, 2000.

Keenan, Jerry. *Encyclopedia of American Indian Wars: 1492–1890.* New York: W. W. Norton, 1997.

Leckie, Robert. *The Wars of America,* vol. 2. New York: HarperCollins, 1992.

Matloff, Maurice, ed. *American Military History,* vol. 1. Conshohocken, Pa.: Combined Books, 1996.

O'Neill, Laurie A. *Wounded Knee: The Death of a Dream.* Brookfield, Conn.: The Millbrook Press, 1993.

Roberts, David. *Once They Moved Like the Wind: Cochise, Geronimo, and the Apache Wars.* New York: Simon & Schuster, 1993.

Trafzer, Clifford E. *The Nez Perce.* New York: Chelsea House, 1992.

Utley, Robert Marshall. *Little Bighorn Battlefield: A History and Guide to the Battle of the Little Bighorn.* Washington, D.C.: Division of Publications, National Park Service, 1994.

Utley, Robert Marshall, and Wilcomb E. Washburn. *The American Heritage History of the Indian Wars.* New York: American Heritage, 1977.

Viola, Herman J. *Little Bighorn Remembered: The Untold Story of Custer's Last Stand.* New York: Times Books, 1999.

———. *It Is a Good Day to Die: Indian Eyewitnesses Tell the Story of the Battle of the Little Bighorn.* New York: Crown, 1998.

Waldman, Carl. *Atlas of the North American Indian* (Rev. ed.) New York: Checkmark Books, 2000.

Wellman, Paul I. *Indian Wars and Warriors.* Boston: Houghton Mifflin, 1959.

INDEX

Page numbers in *italic* indicate photographs or illustrations.